BRITISH PUBS AND INNS

WITH PHOTOGRAPHS FROM
THE FRANCIS FRITH COLLECTION

ST ALBANS, YE OLD FIGHTING COCKS C1960   S2123

BRITISH PUBS AND INNS

WITH PHOTOGRAPHS FROM
THE FRANCIS FRITH COLLECTION

Compiled and edited by Eliza Sackett

Bounty
Books

First published in the United Kingdom in 2006 by The Francis Frith Collection for Bounty Books
a division of Octopus Publishing Group,
2-4 Heron Quays, London E14 4JP, England

Hardback edition ISBN 10: 0-7537-1444-2
ISBN 13: 978-0-7537-1444-7

British Library Cataloguing in Publication Data

British Pubs and Inns
Compiled and edited by Eliza Sackett

The Francis Frith Collection
Frith's Barn, Teffont,
Salisbury, Wiltshire SP3 5QP
Tel: +44 (0) 1722 716 376
Email: info@francisfrith.co.uk
www.francisfrith.com

Designed and assembled by Terence Sackett

Printed in Singapore by Imago

Front Cover: Wargrave, The Village 1890 27177T

CONTENTS

British Pubs and Inns - An Introduction

'I have certainly spent some enviable hours at inns.'
WILLIAM HAZLITT, 'ON GOING A JOURNEY', 1822

The inn has been celebrated in history and literature since medieval times. In inhospitable and often wild and dangerous countryside, it was the only safe haven for the weary traveller. Walking or riding between north and south, east and west, or clattering along in a draughty, uncomfortable coach between remote regions, would have been a daunting and difficult business, and simply reaching your destination would have seemed an achievement. It is hardly surprising that a brightly-lit, comfortable inn became such an enticing prospect. William Hazlitt describes 'how fine it is to enter some old town ... at approach of night-fall, or to come to some straggling village, with the lights streaming through the surrounding gloom; and then, after enquiring for the best entertainment that the place affords, to *take one's ease at one's inn*.'

Like so much that is good in life, we tend to take inns for granted, and it often takes a foreigner to make us perceive their true value. The American traveller Elihu Burritt, during a visit to Britain in the 1860s, noted the extraordinary variety of inns and hostelries: each had 'an individuality as marked as the parish church ... [you will not] find two alike, if you travel from one end of the country to the other. You might as well mistake one of the living animals for the other, as to mistake the Blue Boar for the Red Lion.'

Already, by the 1860s, the inn was an ancient institution, and the heyday of the stage coach had already passed, for the railways were criss-crossing the countryside. Burritt tells how the traditional inn is represented in old engravings:

'with a coach and four drawn up before the door, surrounded by a crowd of spectators and passengers, some descending and ascending on ladders over the forward wheels ... ostlers in long waistcoats, plush or fustian shorts, and yellow leggings, standing bareheaded with watering-pails at the 'osses 'eads; trunks great and small going up and down; village boys in high excitement; the landlord, burly, bland, and happy, with a face as rotund and genial as the full moon; and those round, rosy, sunny, laughing faces peering out of the windows with delightful wonderment and exhilaration, winked at by the driver, and saluted with a graceful motion of his whip-handle in recognition of the barmaid, chambermaid, and all the other maids of the house. The coach, with all its picturesque appointments, its four-in-hand, the stirring heraldry of its horn coming down the road, its rattling wheels, the life and stir aroused and moved in its wake, – all this has gone from the presence of a higher civilization.

It will never re-appear in future pictures of actual life in England.'

The prestigious coaching inn was not usually where working people went for entertainment. In the side streets of towns and along every village street there was invariably a modest public house. Often it did not even declare itself with a signboard, and customers simply walked in to what looked like someone's front room, the landlord serving drinks through a simple hatch. Here the labouring man sought companionship. The naturalist Richard Jefferies writing in the early 1880s explains the importance of such places to rural life:

'The drinking and the smoking are in truth but the attributes of the labourer's public-house evening. It is the conversation that draws him hither ... Any one can drink or smoke alone ... You pass a public-house in the summer evening. You see a number of men grouped about trestle-tables out of doors, and others sitting at the open window; there is an odour of tobacco, a chink of glasses and mugs. You can smell the tobacco and see the ale; you cannot see the indefinite power which holds men there – the magnetism of company and conversation. Their conversation, not your conversation.'

Comfort and conversation seem to be the true heart of the British inn or pub. Elihu Burritt defines its unique quality as 'homefulness', believing that this conjures up the necessary atmosphere of cosiness and quiet. In this oasis of peace you are waited upon, and you gradually sink into a mood of delightful weariness, welcoming the prospects of your evening meal and bed. Hazlitt always relished his nights spent at country inns, enjoying the status of being 'known by no other title than *the gentleman in the parlour*'.

The photographs in this book have been carefully chosen to reflect the extraordinary variety of inns and public houses throughout Britain. Many show the interiors of rooms and bars as they were during the Victorian and Edwardian eras, and up as far as the 1950s – it is likely that most had changed little for centuries. It was only later, during the brave new world of the 1960s, that fashions changed and so much that was old was pulled out and replaced. It is ironic that pub designers today are desperately trying to put it all back, to recreate the unique atmosphere that has drawn travellers and topers down the ages. This book should bring us an insight into the captivating and enduring charm and attraction of the British inn and public house.

Boscastle

The Wellington Hotel, **Boscastle**. The deep inlet of Boscastle's harbour is one of the few safe anchorages on this exposed north coast of Cornwall. Its narrowness and the fact that it is surrounded by high, brooding cliffs of slate and shale make it very difficult to spot from the sea, and a winding inlet has to be negotiated before the harbour can be reached.

Standing near the harbour is the Wellington Hotel; built in the 16th century, it is still in business today. It was one of the last posting houses in the country, with stagecoaches running here up to the 1920s. In 1849 the coach from Saltash took nine hours; it would cost 4s 6d if you rode inside, 3s 4d if you were willing to brave the weather outside. The road journey from Saltash today takes about an hour and a half.

A famous guest of the hotel was the Dorset novelist Thomas Hardy (1840–1928). In 1870 he was still working as an architect, and came here to restore nearby St Juliot's Church. Here he met and fell in love with Emma Gifford, the vicar's sister, whom he married in 1874. In the Wellington Hotel today hang the lamps that Hardy gave to the church.

Launceston

Top: LAUNCESTON, THE SQUARE
AND THE WHITE HART 1906 56132

Above: LAUNCESTON, THE WHITE
HART HOTEL DOOR 1890 23776

The White Hart, Launceston

Launceston is often called the gateway to Cornwall; it crowns the dark hill that rises from the valley of the River Kensey. It boasts a Norman castle, a wealth of historic houses, and a medieval gateway, a remnant of the walls which once enclosed the town. Launceston was always busy on market days. Hotels and pubs such as the White Hart (right) did a brisk trade feeding and watering thirsty farmers and their farm hands. The oval Butter Market was designed by George Wightwick, who also designed the Lower Market House, which still stands in Market Street and is now an arcade. The Butter Market also provided advertising space for all sorts of businesses, from Treleaven's the outfitters to the Great Western Railway. It was demolished in 1919, and the clock with its quarterjacks was transferred to the Guildhall tower.

This was not the first change of address for the quarterjacks: they were carved in 1642, and once adorned the Assize Hall. During their residence in the Square, the quarterjacks were not at all popular with customers at the White Hart, who objected to being woken every fifteen minutes. In 1905 it became the duty of the hotel boots boy to pull and tie down a cord which silenced the quarterjacks during the hours of darkness.

The White Hart dates from the 18th century and has always been at the centre of town life, hosting hunt balls and providing accommodation for the sheriff and his men when the Assizes were in session. The granite doorway is thought to have come from the ruins of St Thomas's Priory. The stag that sat above the doorway was taken down during renovations and mysteriously disappeared, never to be seen again. The gas lamp that lit the entrance is gone, but the holes for its bracket are still visible.

Jamaica Inn, Bolventor

This grey, slate-hung building, once a temperance inn, looks more forbidding than welcoming – its bleak exterior is complemented by a sinister sign (B129037p). In fact, it has long been a welcome stopping point halfway across the desolate Bodmin Moor on the A30 between Launceston and Bodmin; it was probably built in the 18th century, when stagecoaches drew in here on their long journey between London and Falmouth. The stagecoaches were the prey of the villains and highwaymen who haunted this lonely road, and who sat round the inn fireplace along with the coach's passengers. Smugglers probably used this inn too, bringing their contraband from the north or south coasts on the backs of pack ponies along remote moorland tracks – the inn's name is possibly derived from smuggled Jamaica rum. Jamaica Inn became famous after Daphne du Maurier's tale of smuggling was published in 1936, and no doubt these touring motorists were drawn here for that reason. This popular inn complex now bustles with tourists in the summer months.

Bolventor

Top: BODMIN, BOLVENTOR, JAMAICA INN c1950 B129036

Right: BODMIN, THE SIGN, JAMAICA INN c1955 B129037P

The grey slate inn, forbidding and uninhabited

It was a dark, rambling place, with long passages and unexpected rooms. There was a separate entrance to the bar, at the side of the house, and, though the room was empty now, there was something heavy in the atmosphere reminiscent of the last time it was full: a lingering taste of old tobacco, the sour smell of drink, and an impression of warm, unclean humanity packed one against the other on the dark stained benches ... Mary went out on to the road and looked about her, and as far as her eyes could see there was nothing but the black hills and the moors. The grey slate inn, with its tall chimneys, forbidding and uninhabited though it seemed, was the only dwelling-place on the landscape. To the west of Jamaica high tors raised their heads ... FROM 'JAMAICA INN', DAPHNE DU MAURIER 1936

The Keigwin Arms, Mousehole

Mousehole (pronounced 'Mouzel'), three miles from Penzance, is an ancient village: the south pier was first built in around AD400. For centuries it thrived as a fishing port – in the 13th century it was the main port in Mounts Bay – but it lost out with the rise of nearby Newlyn in the 19th century. However, even then there were hundreds of people at work here fishing and packing the fish, and a little fishing is still done here. Dylan Thomas tarried awhile in Mousehole and married his sweetheart Caitlin at Penzance Register Office in 1937. He described Mousehole as 'the loveliest village in England'. Who can argue with that?

The Keigwin Arms, dating from the 14th century, is the oldest building in the village; it takes its name from Jenkin Keigwin, a local squire killed by the Spaniards in July 1595 as he was defending his house – the musket ball that killed him was embedded in the door behind him. The Spaniards sacked the town in revenge for the destruction of the Armada – four galleys had anchored in Mounts Bay, and 200 soldiers attacked the harbours and villages.

A formidable woman

Dolly Pentreath, the last speaker of Cornish as a mother tongue (she died in 1777 aged 102), used to drink flagons of beer and smoke her pipe in the Keigwin Arms. She was a formidable woman – local legend tells that when the press gang landed here to search for men, Dolly chased them back to their boat with a hatchet, cursing them in Cornish.

Below: MOUSEHOLE, THE KEIGWIN ARMS 1893   31805

Mousehole

Lynton

The Valley of the Rocks Hotel, Lynton

Lynton and Lynmouth are situated amidst ravishing scenery where the River Lyn tumbles down from Exmoor to the sea. Originally the home of fishermen, the remote villages found fame in the 1790s when the Romantic poets Coleridge and Wordsworth visited and were entranced by the beauty of what they saw. Other writers, including Hazlitt, Southey, and Shelley, followed, and soon tourists were flocking here, despite the bad roads and steep hills. Every few miles, visitors would have to hire post-horses to pull their carriages, and many of the hotels employed post boys to lie in wait with fresh horses to pull the visitors to the hotel.

In the local North Devon Journal of 19 August 1833, the Valley of the Rocks Hotel (which was established in the early 1800s) was advertised thus: 'The situation of the House is unrivalled, commanding varied views of the Bristol Channel, Valleys of the East and West Lyn, etc. The comfort and quiet of this establishment, (which has been recently enlarged and fitted up with separate suites of apartments,) have ensured it the patronage of the most respectable families in England'. In 1888 the shrewd businessman John Heywood bought the hotel, and allowed the builders of the cliff railway to use part of his land – thus ensuring that guests of the hotel could reach it easily. He demolished the older part of the hotel and built a huge extension; the grandiose architecture and plenteous overstuffed furniture (59374) could not form a greater contrast to the wild scenery outside.

Left: LYNTON,
VALLEY OF THE ROCKS HOTEL 1907 59372

Above: LYNTON, VALLEY OF THE ROCKS HOTEL,
THE LOUNGE 1907 59374

Combe Martin

The King's Arms Hotel, Combe Martin

This fascinating and extraordinary building was built in 1690 and is Grade II listed. Although known as the King's Arms at the time of the photograph it was renamed the Pack of Cards in 1933. There are 4 floors (for the four suits), 13 doors on every floor and 13 fireplaces (for the 13 cards in each suit), and 52 stairs and 52 windows (for the number of cards in a pack) – hence its name. It was built by Squire Ley, who had a passion for gambling, to celebrate a tremendous run of good luck at cards. Inside the pub is a huge trestle table with an unusual, very thick, top. In fact this top is hollow, and young men wishing to escape the press gangs could hide inside. When this photograph was taken the hotel was looking rather run-down, but a major refurbishment has improved it wonderfully.

Clovelly

The New Inn, Clovelly. Clovelly hangs in a cleft in the North Devon cliffs, fringed by luxuriant woodland. It grew organically. The houses were built (mostly of cob) by the fishermen as and when they were needed, and thanks to the precipitous setting, display a remarkable variety of sizes, shapes and styles which somehow manage to harmonise perfectly together. No motor traffic is allowed into the village, and donkeys ply up and down the steep-stepped street, carrying goods on panniers. The New Inn is still there, offering much-needed rest and refreshment to visitors as they near the end of the steep climb up the village street.

Clovelly's remarkable state of preservation, and its unspoilt character, is due to the philanthropic nature of the Hamlyn family, who acquired the manor in 1740. Donkeys were used to transport everything up and down Clovelly's steep street: herring, coal and lime came up the hill from the harbour. The villagers also used sledges to drag groceries and so on up and down the cobbles. The only safe anchorage on the inhospitable, craggy coastline between Appledore and Boscastle, Clovelly lived precariously for centuries from the herring fishery. However, Charles Kingsley used the village as a location in his novel 'Westward Ho!' (1855) – Kingsley's father had been vicar of Clovelly, and Kingsley knew and loved the village well. The book alerted the new breed of holidaymaker to the charm of its steep, cobbled streets; by 1890 there were three hotels.

Left: CLOVELLY, THE NEW INN 1894 33490P

Above: CLOVELLY, THE NEW INN 1923 75159A

Bideford

Kingsley's Rose Salterne

In the mid 20th century the building became the Rose of Torridge tea rooms and restaurant, named after the heroine of Charles Kingsley's 'Westward Ho!' (1855), a book which gave a great boost to tourism in the River Torridge area for many years, and indeed gave its name to the resort of Westward Ho!. In the novel, it is in this tavern that Amyas Leigh and the other suitors of the beautiful Rose Salterne, Rose of Torridge, pledge their loyalty to her and form the Brotherhood of the Rose.

The Old Ship Tavern, Bideford

Bideford, set alongside the beautiful estuary of the twin Rivers Taw and Torridge, is a pleasant market town today, but in medieval times it was one of the busiest and most important ports in Britain. There has been a tavern or restaurant on this site since the 16th century – at that time, this was the end of the original Bideford Quay. Over the years, only the name of the tavern has changed to reflect changing commercial interests. For instance, one of the earliest photographs (taken in 1864) shows it as the Newfoundland Hotel, indicating the importance of the North Atlantic salt cod trade, which brought great wealth to Bideford for over 300 years. These premises still retain a connection with fishing, as they now house a fish restaurant.

Above: BIDEFORD, THE OLD SHIP TAVERN 1906   55928

The Three Crowns Inn, Chagford

Chagford is a tiny market town on the eastern slopes of Dartmoor, close to the upper reaches of the River Teign. With its jumble of streets and pleasing buildings of local granite, it has long been popular with visitors. Alongside the market place is the renowned Three Crowns Inn, a dignified building dating back to the 13th century. The large blocks of granite with which it is built and its two-storey porch give it a feeling of security and solidity.

It was once Whyddon House, the home of the Whyddon family, who lived in Chagford for hundreds of years. In 1641 Mary Whyddon was shot just after her wedding by a jilted suitor; and two years later the Three Crowns saw another shooting. In 1643 (during the Civil War), Parliamentary officers and men were billeted at Whyddon House; meanwhile, a Royalist force was travelling towards the town. Among the Royalists was Sydney Godolphin, the well-born MP for the town of Helston in Cornwall and a poet of renown – his commanding officer described him thus: 'as perfect and as absolute a piece of virtue as ever our nation bred'. There was a skirmish outside the house, in which Godolphin received a mortal wound; he died in the porch of Whyddon House, and was later buried in Okehampton. Some say that his ghost still haunts the rooms of the Three Crowns.

Chagford

Left: CHAGFORD, HIGH STREET 1906 56610

Dartmoor

DARTMOOR, THE WARREN HOUSE INN 1931   84044

The Warren House Inn, Dartmoor

At over 1,400ft above sea level, this has the distinction of being the highest pub in Devon, and the third highest in the country. The inn was cut off from civilisation in 1963 when snowdrifts 20ft high prevented anyone from leaving or reaching it for 12 weeks; supplies had to be dropped in by helicopter. It stands in a remote spot between Two Bridges and Moretonhampstead, two miles from Postbridge, and from it there are wonderful views south over Dartmoor to the south coast. It was originally built to serve the local tin miners – the inn's name refers to the image of three rabbits following each other with their ears joined, the sign of the Vitifer tin mines nearby – and it was allowed to stay open longer than usual because of the miners' long working day. Another reason for the inn's name is the large number of rabbit warrens that were constructed hereabouts.

An Eternal Flame

The Warren House Inn has an unusual claim to fame – the fire there has never gone out since the inn was built in 1845. It was then called the New House, since it replaced another inn on the opposite side of the road. Glowing peat turfs were carried on a shovel from the old inn to the hearth of the new one, and since then the fire has never been allowed to die.

Lydford

The Castle Inn, Lydford

The River Lyd rises high on the moor near Woodcock Hill and eventually joins the Tamar near Lifton. Lydford lies on the western slopes of Dartmoor. It has been inhabited over a very long period, for there is a Bronze Age settlement nearby. It was a Saxon mint town in the time of Ethelred the Unready and a seat of power under Alfred the Great. The castle was built in 1195 – it replaced an earlier timber one. The castle dungeon was used as the Stannary Prison, although Lydford never had the status of Stannary Town.

Conan Doyle called this inn the Albion Inn in 'The Hound of the Baskervilles'. The Castle Inn was built in the year 1550; it is a charming cottage-like building, now painted pink, and the long, low exterior conceals a riot of beams, curios and old furniture in its small, cosy, slate-floored rooms. In the restaurant there is a huge Norman fireplace which is said to have come from the castle next door.

Above: LYDFORD,
THE CASTLE INN 1906 56068

Left: LYDFORD,
THE CASTLE 1906 56070

Gubbins-land

Lydford Gorge (right), the beautiful and romantic ravine, was in the 17th century home to a gang of red-bearded ruffians called the Gubbins who terrorised the locals – eventually they all died 'as a result of intemperance and interbreeding.'

At the time it was said 'Gubbins-land is a Scythia within England, and they pure heathens therein. Their language is the drosse of the dregs of the vulgar Devonian. They hold together like burrs: offend one and all will avenge their quarrel.'

Chudleigh Knighton

CHUDLEIGH KNIGHTON, THE CLAY CUTTERS ARMS 1907   58501

The Clay Cutters Arms, Chudleigh Knighton. This picturesque old inn, its undulating roof covered in slightly threadbare thatch in this photograph, is named after the clay workers who dug out the pipe clay and potters' clay that could be found here; ball clay was mined not far away at nearby Teignwick and Kingsteignton.

The earliest method of transporting the clay was by horse and cart or packhorse; it was taken to Hackney Quay on the River Teign, where cellars were built in the 18th century to store the clay while it was waiting to be loaded onto ships. The vagaries of the tides made shipping the clay down the Teign quite a problem – at low tide the river is reduced to a trickle, so at high tide it would be crowded with all kinds of craft, including Teign barges, with their characteristic flat bottoms, round bows, flat transom sterns, and square sails. Lord Clifford (on whose land in Chudleigh Knighton the clay could be found) built the Hackney Canal, which had a tidal lock at the entrance from the Teign, and a basin next to the clay cellars – this made it far easier to load the boats. Later, a railway line from Newton Abbot was constructed in 1862, providing a better way of transporting the clay.

The George Inn, Norton St Philip

Winding streets fronted by characterful stone cottages of different periods typify this attractive village. Built as their guest house in the 13th century by the Carthusian monks of Hinton Priory, the George Inn catered for the wool merchants who came to the town's two annual fairs: a useful service and a source of income. This famous and most attractive inn has a stone ground floor with two jettied timber-framed upper storeys and fire-proof stone side elevations, while on each gable are rare original lantern-like stone chimneys. Wagons were loaded from the stone platform beside the door (behind the car in this photograph). Samuel Pepys, en route from Salisbury to Bath, came to the George for refreshment and noted in his diary that he 'dined very well for 10s'.

The Duke of Monmouth

The Duke of Monmouth made the inn his headquarters in 1685 and survived an assassination attempt here, only to be defeated by the Royalist forces at the battle of Sedgemoor. Some of his captured troops were imprisoned and held captive in the George in what is now the Dungeon Bar.

Norton St Philip

NORTON ST PHILIP, THE GEORGE INN C1950   N218001

Glastonbury

Above left: GLASTONBURY, THE GEORGE HOTEL AND MARKET CROSS 1890   23907   *Above right:* GLASTONBURY, THE GEORGE HOTEL 1890   23908

The George and Pilgrim Inn, Glastonbury

The town of Glastonbury began as a settlement that grew up outside the abbey. Various servants of the abbey and tradespeople who did business with the monks lived here. Gradually the town grew more important in its own right, acting as a market for the surrounding countryside, especially after Henry VIII's Dissolution of the Monasteries. In a way we still find the abbey here, for after the Dissolution much of the stone of the abbey buildings was re-used in the town. The centrepiece of the square is the Market Cross, designed in 1846 by the ecclesiastical architect Benjamin Ferrey. The cross is in the style of an Eleanor Cross, and it replaced a medieval example.

One building in particular deserves to be picked out from those around the Market Square. It has had several names, but it is now the George and Pilgrim Inn, and is a rare survival of a medieval pilgrim inn. As the name suggests, it was built around 1450 for pilgrims to the abbey by Abbot John Selwood. Local legend has it that Henry VIII watched Glastonbury Abbey burn from one of the inn windows.

Food and shelter

Monastic rules of hospitality meant that the medieval abbeys were obliged to give food and shelter to pilgrims, so hospices were built near the abbeys; these began as single communal rooms with very basic facilities, but many developed into wealthy establishments that survived the Dissolution, as the George and Pilgrim did.

Dulverton

DULVERTON, THE LION HOTEL 1896 37653

The Lion, Dulverton. Dulverton lies on the edge of Exmoor in the valley of the River Barle. Exmoor's tops are good only for sheep, hardy Exmoor ponies and forestry, and gorse, bracken and heather abound. However, surrounding it to the north are steep well-wooded cliffs and combes rising sharply from the sea, while to the east streams and rivers have cut deep valleys and combes, which are also well-wooded and lush: a complete contrast to the plateau. The towns, villages and hamlets occupy these valleys, such as Winsford or Dulverton, the latter now the headquarters of the Exmoor National Park Authority. The highest point is Dunkery Beacon at 1,705ft, but much of the moor is around the 1,500ft mark. It is a very beautiful but wild area; much is made of the 'Lorna Doone' connection, the novel by R D Blackmore set on Exmoor.

   The Lion specialised in accommodation for visitors to the wilds of Exmoor. To the right of the porch is the sign of the Cyclists Touring Club, although the steep lanes leading to the breezy summits would have discouraged many. Anglers fished the racing waters of the Barle, and followers of the hunt congregated in the town's broad street for the regular meets.

The Royal Oak Inn, Winsford. Climbing up from Dulverton, the road crosses typical sheep-grazed Exmoor moorland, bright with yellow gorse flowers and heather, before descending into Winsford in the upper Exe valley. This delightful village of whitewashed cottages focussed on a stream has changed little. The bridge over the stream in the village is an ancient stone slab or 'clapper' bridge of which there are many on Exmoor. It was at Winsford that Ernest Bevin was born in 1881. He became General Secretary of the Transport and General Workers' Union and was later appointed Minister of Labour and then Foreign Secretary.

Originally a 13th-century farm, the Royal Oak became a halt for packhorse trains carrying wool across the hills. Over time a hostelry developed, but only a hundred years ago, a dairy stood where the back bar is today. Tom Faggus, a local highwayman who preyed on visitors to the inn, features in R D Blackmore's 'Lorna Doone'. The Royal Oak's appearance has altered little in the last 70 years, and it continues to provide old-fashioned hospitality in a modern age.

Winsford

Above left: WINSFORD,
THE ROYAL OAK INN 1930 83545

Above right: PORLOCK,
THE SHIP INN 1890 23509P

Verdant Porlock

It was supposedly here in 1798 that the prolific writer, Robert Southey, a close friend of Coleridge and poet laureate from 1807, composed his sonnet on Porlock:

'Porlock, thy verdant vale so fair to sight,
Thy lofty hills, which furze and fern embrown,
The waters that roll musically down
Thy woody glens, the traveller with delight
Recalls to memory, and the channel grey,
Circling its surges in thy level bay ...'

Porlock

The Ship Inn, Porlock. At one time the sea extended to Porlock itself, but a retreating shoreline has left it a mile inland and the harbour is now at Porlock Weir. Standing at the bottom of the notoriously steep climb of Porlock Hill (its summit is 1,400ft above sea level), the Ship Inn appears little changed today, despite the removal of its attractive wooden porches. It was built in 1290 (but considerably altered in the 18th century), and at that time was near the shore, and thus handy for smuggling – it is said that a secret tunnel links the inn to a nearby cottage. In Nelson's time, press gangs came here to force young men into the navy. For centuries the Ship has been at the centre of village life, hosting 'club days' (social events for self-help organisations) and venison feasts for Exmoor stag hunters, for example. In 1840 a toll road was built to bypass steep Porlock Hill, and tolls were taken at the Ship. In 1843 the first stagecoach came through, and from then on two horses were kept at the Ship to help the stagecoach horses climb the hill. While writing 'Kubla Khan', Coleridge was famously interrupted by 'a person from Porlock', and R D Blackmore was another writer connected with Porlock – scenes in his 'Lorna Doone' (1869) are set in the Ship. The authors H G Wells and Rebecca West once stayed here.

Dunster

The Luttrell Arms, Dunster

Dunster, set just a few miles from the Bristol Channel, is one of the most picturesque of Somerset's small towns; its historic watermill was mentioned in Domesday, and its long Market Place rises from the Yarn Market, or market cross, an octagonal structure of 1589, to the castle gatehouse with the castle looming beyond. The imposing Dunster Castle is set in beautiful parkland, and emerges from its tree-girt ridge as one of the most effective compositions in Somerset.

Above: DUNSTER, THE LUTTRELL ARMS AND THE CASTLE C1880 15837

Left: DUNSTER, THE LUTTRELL ARMS, A MANTELPIECE 1888   20900

Now owned by the National Trust, Dunster Castle was the home of the Luttrell family for six centuries, and it was the Luttrells who gave their name to Dunster's most prominent inn. The Luttrell Arms, a beautiful inn built in the 15th century, was used in medieval times as a guest house by the abbots of Cleeve Abbey. Indeed, the beautifully carved oak windows seen in 31237 have a suitably monastic look, and several of the rooms have lofty hammer-beam roofs almost worthy of the abbey itself (see 31235). The huge fireplace has a wonderful 17th-century overmantel (see 20900, page 24).

Left: DUNSTER, THE LUTTRELL ARMS, THE OAK ROOM 1892 31235

Below: DUNSTER, THE LUTTRELL ARMS, OAK WINDOWS 1892 31237

The Smiths Arms, Godmanstone

Godmanstone is situated in the beautiful Cerne valley north of Dorchester. A few miles away is the Cerne Abbas Giant, a huge prehistoric hill figure cut in the chalk. He is naked, boldly priapic and flourishes a club; was he associated with fertility rites? To this day, local lore has it that a woman who wants a baby should visit the giant.

Once the village smithy, the inn at Godmanstone is said to be the smallest public house in England. The flint walls are only about 5ft high to the point where they meet the beautifully thatched roof – its peak is about 12ft high – and the building measures only 20ft by 10ft. It is thought to be about 500 years old. On top of the tiny wooden porch is a gaily-painted sign depicting a blacksmith; the sign reads 'The smallest public house in England, originally a blacksmith's shop. King Charles II stopped here to have his horse shod. He asked for a drink and the smith replied "I have no licence, sir". So there and then the King granted him one.'

Above: GODMANSTONE,
THE SMITHS ARMS C1955 G179003

The Bear and Castle Hotel, Marlborough

Marlborough boasts one of the widest high streets in the country. It is thought the town's name came from 'Maerla's barrow', a burial place, or 'marle burg', meaning chalk town.

There was a settlement here in Roman times, and a Norman castle, and it was a borough by the early 12th century and a prosperous market town. A disastrous fire in the 17th century means that few ancient buildings survive. Now it is famous for its public school, Marlborough College, founded in 1845.

From 1949 the Bear and Castle was known by its present name, the Bear – perhaps it changed its name to avoid confusion with the Castle and Ball. Its front façade faces the High Street (right of photograph), and its side faces the Parade. This exuberant and impressive display of late 19th century architecture is by the prolific and noted architect Crickmay of Weymouth. A dazzling medley of Jacobean and Georgian styles, it presents a bewildering mass of architectural detail; each pair of windows is different on every storey. The Bear and Castle was rebuilt in 1889, but there has been an inn on this site since the 1750s at least.

The Goddard Arms, Swindon

Two hundred years ago Swindon was a quiet and almost unknown market town on a hill in rural north Wiltshire. In the 1830s the Great Western Railway laid its tracks north of the old town close to the Wilts & Berks Canal. Here, the brilliant engineer Isambard Kingdom Brunel established his workshops with housing for the workers. Eventually some 14,000 were employed at the giant complex of the GWR Works.

The Goddard Arms is named after the Goddard family, who owned Swindon's limestone quarries; these quarries had given Swindon an important industry long before the arrival of the GWR, for the stone was considered to be of excellent quality. An inn has stood on this site for 400 years. It was known as the Crown until about 1810, when it was renamed in honour of the Goddard family, the Lords of the Manor of High Swindon. The Magistrates' Court for Swindon was held here until the Old Town Hall was built in the Market Square in 1852.

Marlborough

Swindon

Crime Passionel

In April 1914 Frances Priscilla Hunter, aged 23, a between-maid at the Goddard Arms, was shot dead by her jealous lover, Walter James White. He was executed for the murder at Winchester in June 1914.

Above: MARLBOROUGH, THE BEAR AND CASTLE HOTEL 1906   57184

Left: SWINDON, THE GODDARD ARMS, HIGH STREET 1905   S254605

Salisbury

The Old George Hotel, Salisbury

The Old George Hotel now forms the entrance to the Old George Mall – the remaining upper floors are now disused and closed to the public. This remarkable and ancient building is first recorded in 1378; around that time it belonged to the Teynturer family, who had connections with the Guild of St George – hence the inn's name, perhaps.

The George's impressive frontage dates from the 15th century, and on the upper floor is an unusual 15th-century double hall – the gables form the splendid street façade – and also an earlier 14th-century hall. In the Middle Ages the inn was often used by clergy visiting the cathedral, as it was supposed to be a temperance inn, but the story goes that beer would be smuggled in from the nearby Crown Inn. In the early 17th century a school used part of the building; also, at this time plays were performed in the inn yard.

The two wonderfully atmospheric photographs shown here of the withdrawing room at the George in 1925 are a joy: the genteelly draped lampshades, the dainty flower arrangements and the pretty rococo looking-glasses do ineffectual battle with the dark panelling, the sturdy furniture and the massive ancient timbers.

Samuel Pepys: Our bed good, but lousy …

The diarist Samuel Pepys and his wife stayed here in 1668:
'Came about ten at night to a little Inn, where we were fain to go into a room where a peddler was in bed and made him rise, and here wife and I lay. Good beds and the master of the house a sober, understanding man, and I had good discourse with him about the county's matters as wool and corn and other things. And he also merry and made us mighty merry at supper. Up, finding our bed good, but lousy, which made us all merry'.

Opposite left: SALISBURY,
THE OLD GEORGE HOTEL 1911 63769

Opposite right: SALISBURY, THE OLD GEORGE HOTEL
THE WITHDRAWING ROOM 1928 80916

Above: SALISBURY, THE OLD GEORGE HOTEL
THE WITHDRAWING ROOM 1928 80915

The Old Castle Inn, Old Sarum

Old Sarum, just a mile or two north of present day Salisbury, is set on top of its hill, overlooking the marshy land at the confluence of the Avon and several other rivers draining Salisbury Plain. Old Sarum started life as an Iron Age hill fort; it became the small Roman town of Sorviodunum, a Saxon village, and the site of a Norman castle and cathedral – a small town grew up here in the late 11th century. In the 1220s the site was mostly abandoned in favour of New Sarum, modern Salisbury, and now only ruins of the castle and cathedral remain – but this did not stop it sending a representative to Parliament until 1832!

The Old Castle Inn stands opposite the castle ruins, where the 16th-century historian Leland said there had been 'a fair suburbe' in Norman times, and indeed excavation here has found evidence of a possible church and of cess pits. The photograph of the interior shows everyone's idea of the archetypal pub: horse brasses, coach lanterns, pewter mugs and hunting prints abound, while a fine old settle and a window-seat encourage us to sit around the beamed fireplace for a cosy pint.

Top: OLD SARUM, THE OLD CASTLE INN C1965   O58001   *Above:* OLD SARUM, THE OLD CASTLE INN C1965   O58026

The Ship Hotel, Alveston

Alveston is ten miles from Bristol, and this old coaching inn, where the horses were changed, was the first stop from Bristol, or the last before reaching it. The inn probably dates from the 17th century, and was most likely built on the foundations of an older building, judging by the cellars. Was smugglers' contraband stored here? One of the cellars is known as 'the smuggler's den', and the inn stands only a few miles from the River Severn, where many a cargo of brandy and wine could have been 'run' on dark nights. Upstairs, one of the rooms was a sizeable ballroom in Georgian times. A famous person associated with the inn was Edward Jenner (1749–1823), the pioneer of vaccination; he was a doctor in nearby Berkeley, and a member of the South Gloucestershire Medico-Convivial Society, one of the earliest provincial medical societies in Great Britain, which held its meetings at the Ship.

A Cricketing Heritage

Next to the inn is a cricket pitch; here the famous cricketing brothers, E M and W G Grace, learned to play and astonished all who watched with their prowess.

ALVESTON, THE SHIP HOTEL C1960   A104004

Bucklers Hard

Top: BUCKLERS HARD, THE CHAPEL AND THE HOTEL C1960 B43046

The Master Shipbuilder's House Hotel, Bucklers Hard

This picturesque village, part of the Beaulieu Estate and only two and a half miles from Beaulieu itself, had its beginnings in the early 18th century, when the 2nd Duke of Montagu planned to build a free port, Montagu Town, here. He owned sugar plantations in the West Indies, and he wanted to import and export his sugar. By 1724 plans for a sizeable town had been drawn up, a road to the Beaulieu River constructed, and a few houses built. But his plans came to nothing, and Montagu Town remained a hamlet.

From the late 18th century, the village (now known as Bucklers Hard) found a new role: about 50 wooden ships were built here for the Royal Navy, including three which fought at Trafalgar – the 'Agamemnon' (captained by Nelson in 1783 and his favourite ship), the 'Eurylus', and the 'Swiftsure'. These cottages were the homes of the shipwrights, and the Master Shipbuilder, Henry Adams, lived in the handsome house at the end of the row beside the Beaulieu River. With the advent of iron ships, Bucklers Hard became a sleepy village again, popular with yachtsmen.

Since 1926 the Master Shipbuilder's house has been a hotel; inside is Henry Adams's workroom, complete with plans and models of ships, its window looking out over his shipyard and the river where his ships sailed down to the Solent. The hotel is a mellow, dignified building, with big sash windows, a tiled roof, and a porticoed door.

The White Horse Hotel, Romsey

It was wool and brewing that put Romsey on the map, and several mills were established on the picturesque streams and watercourses of the River Test, which is fed by clear springs under the chalk soil and has long been renowned for its fine trout fishing. Romsey is known for its associations with two distinguished Englishmen: Admiral of the Fleet Earl Mountbatten of Burma and Lord Palmerston, the Conservative Prime Minister during Queen Victoria's reign, both lived here.

The White Horse (49336, below, far right) has been an important inn in Romsey Market Place for many centuries. The present building, largely timber-framed, dates from Tudor times and has Tudor wall paintings, but there is evidence in the cellars of an even earlier building. It has always been used by the local inhabitants as well as by travellers. This was particularly so in the case of property auctioneers and the market fraternity in the 19th century.

In the heyday of the coaching era in the mid 18th century, the White Horse had thirty-five beds, six rooms, and stabling for fifty horses and room for four carriages. Although the much-enlarged modern hotel has thirty-three bedrooms now, thirty-five beds did not mean thirty-five bedrooms three hundred years ago. There were probably one or two dormitory-style rooms, and staff slept over the stables or where they worked. Behind the photographer were the livery stables, now converted to hotel accommodation. At that time the stables were the home of the horse that pulled the trap carrying customers to and from the railway station and also pulled the fire engine when the fire service was called to an emergency.

Romsey

Differing opinions of Romsey amongst travellers

A Dr John Latham, writing about Romsey in 1820, said: 'This town is on a leading road to the west and a good thoroughfare with good inns viz the White Horse which is the principal one. The public is accommodated with post chaises and horses, besides which stage coaches pass daily to London, Portsmouth, Southampton, Salisbury and from the latter to Bath, Bristol and many other places westward.' The traveller John Byng was not so complimentary during his journey to the west in 1782: 'No information of my road could be got here, so I must proceed by map as a mariner does by his compass; for neither ostler nor waiter knew a mile from the door, and a landlord would scorn to wait upon me.'

Bishop's Waltham

The Crown Inn, Bishop's Waltham. Bishop's Waltham, which first grew up in medieval times, is situated twelve miles east of Winchester. It gets its name from Henry of Blois, Bishop of Winchester and brother of King Stephen, who built the bishop's palace here in the 12th century. The bishops of Winchester were not just men of the church but important political figures; guests at the palace included Henry V, who stayed here on his way to the Battle of Agincourt, and Mary Tudor, who waited here for the arrival of her future husband, Philip II of Spain. In 1644, during the Civil War, Cromwell destroyed the palace, but its ruins can be visited today. The fine church was built in Norman times. The picturesque Crown Inn dates from the early 16th century. Photographs B612044 and B612046 give us a wonderful impression of a relatively early example of pub theming. A tremendous variety of weapons is on display, but the suits of armour look almost forbidding – could one eat, drink and be merry in their presence? The pleasant, low-ceilinged, panelled room is typical of the 16th century.

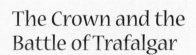

The Crown and the Battle of Trafalgar

A fascinating moment in the Crown Inn's history occurred during the Napoleonic Wars. After the battle of Trafalgar, about 200 French prisoners of war were sent to Bishop's Waltham, and Admiral Villeneuve, the commander of the French fleet, was held at the Crown Inn.

So was the artist Ambrose Louis Garneray, who painted several of his marine pictures here. He spent the next nine years confined in the prison hulks off Portsmouth, and wrote a remarkable record of the daily life of the prisoners of war. After his release in 1814, he became one of France's most distinguished marine painters.

Top left: BISHOP'S WALTHAM,
THE CROWN INN, THE ARMOURY BAR C1955 B612046
Top right: BISHOP'S WALTHAM,
THE CROWN INN, THE COURTYARD C1955 B612070
Above: BISHOP'S WALTHAM, THE CROWN INN, THE ARMOURY BAR
C1955 B612044

Hambledon

The Bat and Ball, Hambledon

This is a holy of holies for cricket lovers, for the Bat and Ball at Broadhalfpenny Down stands opposite a cricket pitch, one of the oldest in the country, and a huge granite monument bearing the inscription: 'This marks the site of the ground of the Hambledon Cricket Club circa 1750–1787'.

During cricket matches, the inn was used as the pavilion and clubhouse. The Cricket Club's secretary (and the formulator of many of the rules of the game still in force today) was Richard Nyren, landlord of the inn. It was at this ground in 1777 that Hambledon roundly beat an all-England team by an innings and 168 runs. It is said that the victorious team celebrated with a drink of punch strong enough 'to make a cat speak'.

Left: HAMBLEDON, THE BAT AND BALL C1955   H405017

Christina Willes – pioneer of around-arm bowling

In 1787, ten years after the Hambledon cricket team's redoubtable victory, the Marylebone Cricket Club, the MCC, was formed by the president of the Hambledon Cricket Club.

It was at Hambledon, too, in 1807 that Christina Willes 'to avoid entanglement with her voluminous skirt, bowled around-arm to a batsman of Hambledon, and thus started such bowling in due course for all who played the game'.

John Nyren, son of Richard and also landlord of the inn, in his fascinating book 'The Cricketers of My Time' (1833), wrote: 'No eleven in England could compare with the Hambledon ... So renowned a set were the men of Hambledon, that the whole country round would flock to see them on their trial matches'.

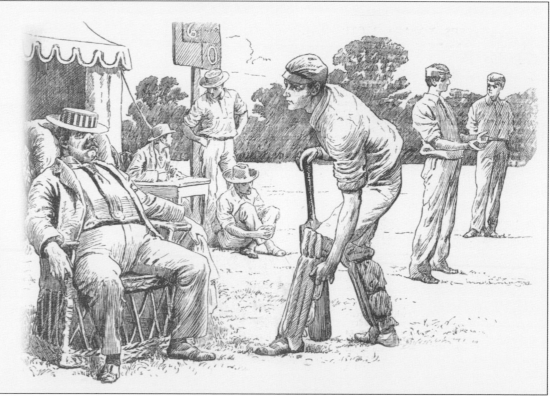

Hurstbourne Tarrant

HURSTBOURNE TARRANT, THE GEORGE AND DRAGON, ANDOVER ROAD C1955
H417004

HINDHEAD,
THE ROYAL HUTS HOTEL 1906 55507

The George and Dragon, Hurstbourne Tarrant

This picturesque village, with its long winding street, was the subject of Anna Lea Merritt's 'A Hamlet in Old Hampshire' (1902), and to this day, it remains the quintessential English village. It is also the meeting point for two of Hampshire's smaller, lesser-known waterways – the Bourne rivulet and the River Swift. A long main street, groups of thatched cottages, and a picturesque 17th-century coaching inn at the foot of a steep hill create an atmosphere of charm and quiet dignity. The writer William Cobbett regarded it as his favourite village – 'a sight worth going many miles to see', he claimed.

There were once five coaching inns here, and the George and Dragon, which dates from the 16th century, is the sole survivor. This inn still preserves the letter rack where letters brought by the coaches were kept until they were collected. The horses that drew the coaches needed to be changed often, and sometimes had to be helped by a local farmer's carthorse, for this village is situated near the formidably steep Hurstbourne Hill.

Hindhead

The Royal Huts Hotel, Hindhead. Surrey's high heaths continue into the south west around Hindhead and Haslemere, where holidaymakers flock to gaze at the splendid valley of the Devil's Punchbowl. The Hindhead crossroads on the busy A3 were named after this hotel, which at one time had been an isolated hut on the Portsmouth Road from which bilberries or whortleberries were sold to travellers. (The berries, which still grow locally, were used as a source of dye.)

In 'Frensham Then and Now' (Baker and Minchin, 1938) we are told that 'as to the buildings called 'The Hut', now known to us as the Huts Hotel, it is safe to say that they constituted one of the oldest habitations on Hindhead, comprising a little inn of a very primitive type, with a brewery attached. The brewery, now dismantled, was in action as recently as 1870, John Elliston being the last to brew ale there'. Travellers would have been glad to find shelter in this inn, for in the 19th century the surrounding area was wild and lawless: 'It is equally certain that up to the middle of the [19th] century many of the squatters who sparsely inhabited the Hindhead valleys … eked out a hand-to-mouth existence by sheep stealing and highway robbery. They were frequented too by fugitives from justice, from whose depredations nothing in the immediate vicinity was safe'. Alas, in the motor age the Royal Huts became a Happy Eater restaurant, and since then the site has been developed for housing – a far cry from the untamed wilderness that Hindhead used to be.

Thursley

Above: THURSLEY, THE RED LION 1907   57522

The Red Lion, Thursley

In the 18th century the Red Lion was a popular stopping point on the London to Portsmouth road before the stage coaches began the long haul up to the wild and treacherous wastes of Hindhead Common, the second highest point in the county.

In September 1786 this inn was a final supping place for an unknown sailor who was subsequently robbed and murdered by his three Irish companions on the heights above. The villains were pursued by a posse of ten or eleven men from the Red Lion; the posse captured the villains near Petersfield, and they were convicted and hung on Gibbet Hill, Hindhead in April 1787. The sailor lies buried in Thursley churchyard, while the inn is now a privately owned house.

Right:
ALBURY, THE
DRUMMOND ARMS
1924 75299A

The Drummond Arms, Albury

The original site of the village of Albury was within Albury Park; the village was moved west and south of the Tillingbourne from the late 18th century onwards, when Admiral Finch bought the mansion and developed the park around it by persuading the villagers to move (or harassing them) and diverting the roads. Subsequent owners of Albury Park continued the process up to the 1850s. The Drummond Arms is named after the banker Henry Drummond, who had a new parish church built for the villagers to replace the old Saxon church, which was closed in 1841. Henry Drummond was a major figure in the story of Albury in Victorian times. He was twice a Member of Parliament, and he reconstructed the mansion in Albury Park where he lived. His daughter married the 6th Duke of Northumberland, and much of the land still belongs to the Northumberland family.

Above: ALBURY, THE DRUMMOND ARMS 1922 71800

The well-dressed patrons of the Drummond Arms in the above photograph appear to be drinking nothing stronger than tea, refreshing on a hot summer day. The charming gardens behind the inn run down to the River Tillingbourne. Albury's name may derive from 'Alderbury' – many alders grow on the riverbanks.

Dorking

The White Horse Hotel, Dorking

'Dorking is one of those old pleasant little towns which have a special character of their own; one of those which are a blend of all that is home-like, lovely and beautiful in England.' So says the 'Rambler's Guide to Dorking and Environs' (c1930). 'Tales of Old Inns' (2nd ed 1929) adds: 'The White Horse at Dorking has always been a patrician among English inns, the great coaching house of the place with its dozens of bedrooms, its scores of servants, and its vast range of stables', and the book paints a vivid picture of what it must have been like in coaching days: 'You can almost hear to-day, echoing back from its white walls, the notes of the horn and the clatter of hoofs on the cobbles, as the Worthing Accommodation rattled in, five hours out from the Belle Sauvage on Ludgate Hill, or the Dorking stage from the Spread Eagle in Gracechurch Street pulled up at the end of its 23-mile journey.'

The White Horse is a very old inn. Its first name was the Cross House, referring to its former owners, the Knights of St John of Jerusalem, whose badge was a Maltese cross. They are said to have bought it from the Knights Templar in 1278; certainly the cellars, carved out of the sandstone on which Dorking stands, are very old, and from them a passage leads down to an ancient well. The building we see today dates from the 15th century, with the long street frontage probably built in the early 18th century. Through the old archway is the cobbled stable yard, and beyond is a large garden.

Opposite above: DORKING, THE WHITE HORSE HOTEL C1960   D45072

Opposite below: DORKING, HIGH STREET AND THE WHITE HORSE 1905   53333

Above: DORKING, HIGH STREET AND THE WHITE HORSE 1932   84974

Sam Weller patronises the Marquis of Granby in Dorking

Dickens visited here often, and in his 'Pickwick Papers' it was in Dorking that Sam Weller descended from the Arundel coach and headed for the fictional Marquis of Granby, kept by Mrs Weller – Dickens's original for this pub was probably the King's Head.

'It was just seven o'clock when Samuel Weller, alighting from the box of a stage-coach which passed through Dorking, stood within a few hundred yards of the Marquis of Granby. It was a cold, dull evening; the little street looked dreary and dismal; and the mahogany countenance of the noble and gallant marquis seemed to wear a more sad and melancholy expression than it was wont to do, as it swung to and fro, creaking mournfully in the wind. The blinds were pulled down, and the shutters partly closed; of the knot of loungers that usually collected about the door, not one was to be seen; the place was silent and desolate.'   FROM 'PICKWICK PAPERS' 1837

Burford Bridge

BOX HILL, THE BURFORD BRIDGE HOTEL 1922   71814

Burford Bridge Hotel, Box Hill. This hotel nestles at the foot of Box Hill, and has a surprisingly rich history. It began its life in 1254, when it was called the Fox and Hounds; part of the present building dates back to the 16th century, and incorporates wooden beams taken from ships of the Spanish Armada.

In 1882 the hotel was known both as the Hare and Hounds and as the Burford Bridge; it finally became the Burford Bridge Hotel in 1905. Lord Nelson, along with Lady Hamilton, spent his last night ashore here in 1805, before travelling on to Portsmouth and embarking on HMS 'Victory' for the battle of Trafalgar. In a second floor bay-windowed room overlooking the garden John Keats completed his epic poem 'Endymion' in November 1817. Jane Austen stayed here too (a picnic at Box Hill is immortalised in her novel 'Emma', 1816), and so did the playwright Sheridan and the poet Wordsworth. Queen Victoria was a guest here as a girl, and the writer Robert Louis Stevenson was also a frequent visitor.

Joy to live in such a place!

John Keats (1795–1821) found London dull, and came to Surrey for inspiration. He finished his poem 'Endymion' after a walk in the moonlight. He wrote home to his mother: 'There is a hill and a dale, and a little river – went up Box Hill this evening after the moonrise ... Came down again and wrote some lines'. After a long walk along the River Mole, he expressed his delight in the Surrey countryside: 'O thou would'st joy to live in such a place'.

Friday Street

BOX HILL, THE BURFORD
BRIDGE HOTEL 1906
55718A

The Stephan Langton, Friday Street

One of the small iron-working hamlets in the valley of the Tilling Bourne, Friday Street probably derives its name from the Scandinavian goddess Frigga; it still enjoys its peaceful setting above a tranquil hammer pond surrounded by steep pine-covered slopes. The dictionary defines a hammer pond as an artificial pond by a water mill; in the 11th century the Wotton mill stood here, grinding corn. Later, iron, wire and gunpowder were made here – the powder mill was established in the reign of Henry VIII. The mill had gone by the mid 18th century.

Above: FRIDAY STREET, THE STEPHAN LANGTON 1921 69984

The Stephan Langton Inn is named after the Archbishop of Canterbury who was one of the three signatories of the Magna Carta in June 1215, and who was, according to legend, born here. The pub's aspidistra and another indoor plant have been transported outside for some fresh air, alongside the footpath leading to the top of Leith Hill (see drawing).

Right:
BLETCHINGLEY,
THE HUNT AT
YE OLDE WHYTE
HARTE HOTEL C1965
B122081

Below:
BLETCHINGLEY,
A CHIMNEY CORNER
AT YE OLDE WHYTE
HARTE 1907 57494

Ye Olde Whyte Harte Hotel, Bletchingley

Bletchingley lies to the east of Redhill. The houses in the High Street date from the 16th to the 20th century. Before 1582, documents referred to this village as 'Blechingley', and even today some residents are opposed to the introduction of the 't' into its name. The origins of the village probably date back to the 7th or 8th centuries, and the name probably means 'the ley (or clearing) of the Blaecci people'.

The top photograph shows eager hounds clustered around the door of Ye Olde Whyte Harte Hotel; this venerable landmark (refronted and white stuccoed in the 1700s) has been an inn since 1388 – it is said to be built from ships' timbers that were 400 years old even then. Note the ornate wrought iron inn sign on the left.

Inside the inn, there are no fewer than three impressive old fireplaces. The one in photograph 57494 is known as the chimney corner; note the fire-back in the grate dated 1613, the splendid firedogs, the cauldrons and warming pans, and the cosy seats where one can toast one's toes. Next to the fireplace in a back room is an old bread oven.

Caterham

The Railway Hotel, Caterham

Caterham is in two parts, up the hill where the medieval church is, and Caterham Valley to the east on the valley floor, which grew up when the railway arrived in 1856 – it was in fact a terminus station. Thus the lower town is Victorian in character, with later suburbs, and its church, St John's, dates from the 1880s.

The exuberant Tudoresque architecture of the Railway Hotel reflects the optimism of the railway age. This is a large hotel, big enough to accommodate plenty of travellers on the railway, and needing plenty of supplies, as the tradesmen's vehicles outside testify.

Above: CATERHAM, THE RAILWAY HOTEL 1894   34290

Fittleworth

The Swan Hotel, Fittleworth

Fittleworth is situated in West Sussex, just to the north of the South Downs. Parts of this pleasant, tile-hung inn date from the 15th century, or even earlier. During the coaching days of the 18th century it was a posting house with large stables behind – note the high, wide passageway in the right-hand part of the building (66921). By the early 1900s the Swan was described as 'a venerable and rambling building', popular with cyclists, motor car enthusiasts and particularly artists, many of whom decorated the Swan's little parlour with their paintings.

The photographs of the interior give a wonderful impression of how Victorian and Edwardian styles struggle ineffectually against the older structure of the building. Ferns, potted palms and aspidistras flourish, gas lamps are suspended from walls and ceilings, damask, lace and cleverly-folded napkins abound, and a velvet cloth with a bobble fringe covers the mantelshelf in a genteel manner – but nothing can obliterate the dignity of old beams and well-proportioned rooms.

Opposite above:
FITTLEWORTH,
THE SWAN HOTEL
1914 66921

Opposite below:
FITTLEWORTH,
THE SWAN HOTEL
C1950 F29003

Left:
FITTLEWORTH,
THE SWAN HOTEL,
THE PICTURE ROOM
1921 70078

Below left:
FITTLEWORTH,
THE SWAN HOTEL,
THE VERANDA 1920
66927

England's celebrated painter

The painter John Constable is said to have stayed here – he frequently painted this beautiful area, which continues to attract artists. He was also a regular visitor to nearby Brighton.

Arundel

ARUNDEL, THE BLACK RABBIT 1898 42551P

The Black Rabbit, Arundel

Overlooking the pretty River Arun near Arundel, the Black Rabbit was first licensed in 1804; at that time it was a popular watering-hole for the workers who were building the railway and digging a new cut of the river. Several years after this photograph was taken, it became a fashionable haunt of Edwardians. Today the Black Rabbit is popular with riverside walkers and those visiting the nearby Wildfowl and Wetlands Trust reserve, with its 60 acres of ponds, lakes and reed beds and over 1,000 species of ducks, geese and swans. The Black Rabbit's restaurant was once the old boat houses.

Billingshurst

Ye Olde Six Bells, Billingshurst

Billingshurst is one of the larger villages in Sussex. It may get its name from the Saxon 'Billings', meaning 'wooded hill in the territory of Billa's people', or perhaps from the Roman engineer Belinus who was responsible for Stane Street, the Roman road linking London with Chichester. Stane Street eventually enters London at Billingsgate, so a Roman origin for the names of both places seems possible.

The coaching trade was important to the village in the 18th and early 19th centuries. This inn stands in the centre of the village by the side of the main London to Worthing road on the route of Stane Street; it is said to date back to the 14th century. It is a timber-framed building with a Horsham stone roof, and it has an unusual overhang along the whole length of the first floor. This inn has had a long and varied history. In 1530 it was a farmhouse and subsequently a coach house; it was a tannery in 1830 and a brewery in 1851.

To us today, the pub interior shown in 74919 seems almost spartan. Where are the fibreglass beams, the deep-pile carpet, the reproduction antique tables and chairs, the hunting prints, and the horse brasses? However, this plain room has undeniable charm. Note the random yet harmonious mix of old furniture – the settle, the bench, the tables – and the gas light. A beautiful old inglenook fireplace is hiding under the gloss paint; did the cupboards inside it once hold salt and other comestibles that needed to be kept dry? The slow tick of the clock and the newspaper encourage us to sit for a while with a relaxing pint.

Above left: BILLINGSHURST, YE OLDE SIX BELLS 1923 74918

Below left: BILLINGSHURST, YE OLDE SIX BELLS, AN OLD FIREPLACE 1923 74919

Crawley

Crawley's George Hotel is reputed to be haunted by the ghost of Mark Hewton, a night porter who liked to deliver wine to guests in the evening, regardless of whether they wanted it or not. Any wine left over when he collected it, he would consume himself. Unfortunately for him, one guest had put poison in some of this wine, which Hewton drank and promptly died. Staff insist that they have unpleasant feelings in the locality of his room, now No 7, and say they have seen faint shapes. They have also had trouble with the corridor lights, which frequently turn themselves on and off.

The George Hotel, Crawley

In 1810, when the London to Brighton daily mail coach began, Crawley became a 'post town' - it formed an important staging post where horses were changed. The George Hotel was a famous coaching inn. One of the best descriptions of how it would have looked back in its Regency heyday can be found in Sir Arthur Conan Doyle's novel 'Rodney Stone' (1896): 'And then at last, we saw the formless mass of the huge Crawley elm looming before us in the gloom, and there was the broad village street with the glimmer of the cottage windows, and the high front of the old George Inn, glowing from every door and pane and crevice, in honour of the noble company who were to sleep within that night.' The hotel name derives from St George rather than the Prince Regent, who is said to have been a regular visitor on his way to Brighton.

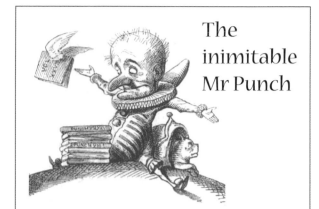

The inimitable Mr Punch

An important Crawley resident was the first editor of Punch, Mark Lemon, who was almost solely responsible for developing the town's urban society. Vine Cottage, where Mark Lemon lived with wife Nelly and their large family, stood where Asda does now. In the year 2000 a plaque in his memory was put up outside the George Hotel, where he had held Punch editorial meetings.

Opposite above: CRAWLEY, THE GEORGE HOTEL 1903   50758   *Opposite below:* CRAWLEY, THE GEORGE HOTEL C1955   C182002

Forest Row

The Swan, Forest Row

Forest Row, recorded in the early 14th century, lies three miles south west of East Grinstead on the verge of Ashdown Forest. Music and bell ringing in the village greeted the Governor General of India, Lord Ellenborough, on his way to Kidbrooke in 1844. Forest Row grew after the arrival of the railway in 1866, and became a parish in 1894. This Ashdown Forest village grew up on the site of royal hunting lodges.

The Swan, which dates back to the Middle Ages, was originally an ale house serving cattle drovers, packhorse men – and smugglers! Most of the present building dates from the 18th and 19th centuries, when the inn (then known as the Yew Tree, after a nearby yew) was a busy coaching inn on the London-Brighton turnpike via Tunbridge Wells.

Right: FOREST ROW, THE SWAN 1907   57957

Alfriston

The Star Inn, Alfriston

Alfriston's much-loved High Street, home to two of its famous hostelries, is little changed today. The 15th-century George Inn, on the right of the photographs, has some Tudor wall paintings. On the left is the superb timber-framed Star Inn, one of the oldest inns in England, whose exterior is decorated with woodcarvings of beasts. It was originally a hospice attached to Battle Abbey and called the Star of Bethlehem – here pilgrims could stay on their journey to the shrine of St Richard at Chichester.

Alfriston was originally a Saxon settlement beside the River Cuckmere. The alarming lion figurehead (shown in detail in photograph A33029), which still stands outside the Star Inn, may have come from a Dutch warship which was wrecked nearby in the 1800s and was pounced upon by Stanton Collins and his smugglers; another theory is that it came from a Dutch warship sunk by the Duke of York in 1672 during the battle of Sole Bay off East Anglia.

Smugglers! *In the 1800s Alfriston was a base for a gang of smugglers notorious for their violence – another pub in the village, the Smugglers Inn, was once the home of the leader, Stanton Collins. Collins was caught stealing sheep in the 1830s, and was transported to Australia.*

Left: ALFRISTON, HIGH STREET AND THE STAR AND GEORGE INNS 1891 28392

Above: ALFRISTON, HIGH STREET AND THE STAR AND GEORGE INNS 1921 71422P

Top: ALFRISTON, THE FIGUREHEAD OUTSIDE THE STAR INN C1955 A33029

Rye

The Mermaid Inn, Rye

Rye, set on its sandstone isle rising from the flat fen of Romney Marsh, still presents something of a medieval picture, dominated by the great church of St Mary. Rye became a member of the Cinque Ports confederation in 1191, at first as a 'limb' of Hastings. In 1336, it was styled an 'Ancient Town'. It suffered much in the raids of the Hundred Years' War. The old hospital (dating from 1576), on the right in Mermaid Street (21161), so called since it performed that function during the Napoleonic Wars, forms the main subject of this early picture of the most photographed of Rye's cobbled streets which slopes downhill towards Strand Quay. Its historic buildings, ranging from medieval half-timbering to Georgian brick, are well preserved today.

The Mermaid, one of the 17 public houses in Rye, is a very ancient inn. It was well established in 1420, when it had to be rebuilt after a French raid, and it has always been a haven for travellers. An archway in the façade leads into the courtyard and stabling for the stagecoach horses. The hotel has a vaulted undercroft, which was used as a storehouse by the smuggling gangs of the marshes – in the 18th century Rye was in the grip of the Hawkhurst Gang, ruthless smugglers, who made the Mermaid their headquarters and defied the law. How fitting it is that Russell Thorndyke made the Mermaid the setting of his Dr Syn novels, stories of a smuggling parson.

Above: RYE, MERMAID INN 1912 64930   *Opposite above:* RYE, MERMAID STREET 1888 21161   *Opposite below:* RYE, MERMAID HOTEL 1901 47456

Ightham

The George and Dragon Inn, Ightham

This delightful rambling village may have acquired its name from the Saxon king Ehta, or perhaps from the Saxon words for 'Otha's settlement'. This village was anciently known as Eightham, and was once a market town, with a Whit-Wednesday fair called Cockscomb Fair. Nearby Ightham Mote is a secluded 15th-century manor house with a moat refreshed by natural springs. Ightham's grocer's shop was formerly run by the noted local archaeologist Benjamin Harrison (1837–1921), who achieved international recognition in the Victorian era for his archaeological work hereabouts; he was responsible for the discovery of numerous early flint tools in the vicinity. He died at the age of 84, and is commemorated in a tablet in the local church.

To the left of these photographs is the beautiful half-timbered frontage of the George and Dragon inn, a fine example of Tudor architecture dating from 1515. It is said that it was the home of the Earl of Stafford and that Elizabeth I visited here. Behind the George and Dragon's free-standing sign in photograph 47623 is the Railway Bell Inn. Photograph 14006 shows that the building maintained a connection with transport, for in the 1950s it was a garage! It also shows that beneath the Railway Bell's roughcast is some splendid half-timbering.

The hatching of the Gunpowder Plot

The house next door to the George and Dragon Inn was where the Gunpowder Plot was hatched, and local legend has it that the Duke of Northumberland was imprisoned here after the discovery of the plot. It is also believed that Guy Fawkes stayed here the night before the attempt to carry out the plot.

Left: IGHTHAM, THE SQUARE 1901 47623
Above: IGHTHAM, THE SQUARE C1950 14006

Goudhurst

The Star and Eagle, Goudhurst

Standing near the top of a hill overlooking the Weald, the Star and Eagle is a fine half-timbered mainly 15th-century inn adjoining the churchyard. It was once part of a medieval monastery; it is possible to see the remains of 14th-century stone vaulting inside the inn, and an underground passage led from the inn cellars to the church next door. Next door is the weather-boarded Eight Bells. In the 18th century, the Star and Eagle was the favoured inn of the local smugglers – the fearsome gang intimidated the whole district, to the extent that the villagers, refusing to be bullied any longer, fought a pitched battle with them. The smugglers were defeated, and their ringleader was hanged at nearby Horsemonden Heath.

It is hardly surprising that inns proliferate hereabouts, for this part of Kent was a great hop-growing area. Hop production was once very labour intensive, particularly when harvesting began on 1 September. With the decline in the rural population, whole families would come down from the East End of London to harvest the hop bines. This would give them a much-needed income, and also an annual break in the unpolluted countryside. The newly installed railway connection serving the Weald of Kent had no doubt dropped many of the workers seen in 52571 off to start work in the hop fields. They all seem relaxed enough to pose for the camera as they weigh in their bushels for the farmer. A hundred years later much of their hard work would be replaced by machines. Hop production was once widespread in Kent, but is now located around the Paddock Wood area, where the extensive Whitbread Hop Farms and the headquarters of the Hop Marketing Board are located.

Above: GOUDHURST, THE STAR AND EAGLE C1955   G38062

Right: GOUDHURST, MEASURING THE HOPS 1904   52571

Dartford

The Crown and Anchor Inn, Dartford

This restored medieval house, on the corner of Bullace Lane, is traditionally believed to have been the home of the Kentish rebel Wat Tyler, leader of the Peasants' Revolt of 1381. An insolent tax collector is said to have indecently assaulted Tyler's daughter whilst at the house collecting payment, and was killed by Tyler with a hammer when he heard about it. Tyler became a popular hero, and went on to lead an uprising against serfdom, the hated poll tax, and other grievances. The rebels met with the young king, Richard II, at Smithfield, where Tyler was wounded by William Walworth, Mayor of London. Tyler was taken to St Bartholomew's Hospital, but Walworth had him dragged away and beheaded.

DARTFORD, THE CROWN AND ANCHOR INN C1955 D3069

The Spaniards Inn, Hampstead

DICK TURPIN

Dick Turpin stayed here and stabled his horse across the road. Spaniards Road cuts across the north part of Hampstead Heath; it is a straight 18th-century turnpike road with the toll house surviving opposite the Spaniards Inn. This 18th-century pub and the toll house (extreme left) formed the entrance to the Bishop of London's Hornsey estate.

Little in the photograph has drastically altered, except that the semi-circular arch has gone from what is now the car park entrance, and the rather fine pub sign has also disappeared. The pinch-point in the road caused the local council to toy with the idea of demolishing the listed toll house in the 1970s, but local opinions were listened to, and it remains today. Behind the pub is Evergreen Hill, the house of Dame Henrietta Barnett (1851–1936), the founder of Hampstead Garden Suburb.

The Spaniards Inn is said to have been founded either by the Spanish Ambassador's valet – the Spanish Ambassador stayed here when he retreated from London during an outbreak of the plague – or by two Spanish brothers who killed each other in a duel.

Hampstead

HAMPSTEAD HEATH, THE SPANIARDS INN C1890 L130095

Hampstead

HAMPSTEAD HEATH, THE OLD BULL AND BUSH, NORTH END ROAD 1898   41581

The Bull and Bush, Hampstead

Hampstead Heath, extending from Kenwood House in the north to an area around Parliament Hill in the south, occupies some 800 acres. It has been popular with artists and authors since the 18th century. The Bull and Bush is said to have been built as a farm in the mid 17th century, and it was licensed in 1721. The bull of the pub's name alludes to the farm, and the bush was a yew bush, said to have been planted by William Hogarth, the painter, who stayed here during the summers and laid out the garden – see his portrayal of the delights of beer to the right.

Among those who drank here were the painters Joshua Reynolds and Thomas Gainsborough, and also David Garrick, the actor, playwright and theatre manager. The building we see in this photograph seems to be an atmospheric dream pub, with its low doorway stepping down into a dark panelled bar. At the time the photograph was taken, Florrie Forde, the music hall star, had made the pub famous with her well-known song: ' … Come, come, come and make eyes at me, down at the Old Bull and Bush …'. The pub's popularity at this time was due to Henry Humphries, landlord in 1867, who organised sing-songs and concerts, which continued into the Edwardian period. The pub was reconstructed in 1924 and refurbished in the 1980s.

William Hogarth and 18th-century drinking

Hogarth's horrific illustration showing the terrible effects of gin addiction on the London poor is unforgettable. However, in his 1750 illustration 'Beer Street' (right) he sought to depict a different view of alcohol: we see how good English beer, in moderation, could be drunk and enjoyed by all.

The George, **Southwark**. The George, London's only surviving galleried inn (now in the care of the National Trust) stands in a courtyard off Borough High Street – we can see the now lost archway to the High Street in this photograph. Borough High Street used to be lined with inns, for it was an important route in medieval times, leading to the main bridge over the Thames in one direction and Canterbury in the other – this was the pilgrims' road, busy day and night, always crowded with travellers needing rest and refreshment. The Southwark inns were and remain famous; Chaucer's pilgrims set out from the Tabard, and Shakespeare and Dickens wrote of the White Hart.

Like them, the George has long been part of the fabric of London life, and Dickens wrote of it in 'Little Dorrit'. It was shown on a map of 1542, but an inn probably stood here long before that. It was originally built round three sides of a courtyard, and from its balconies the inn's guests could watch plays performed by travelling troupes of actors – those were the days before theatres existed. Shakespeare himself, who lived in Southwark, may well have come here to see his own plays, and those by other authors. The old inn burned down in 1676, but it was immediately rebuilt in the same style, and remained unchanged until the 19th century, when it was partly torn down to make room for offices for the Great Northern Railway. Today this beautifully restored building still functions as an inn.

GEOFFREY CHAUCER

SOUTHWARK, THE GEORGE INN C1875   L130130

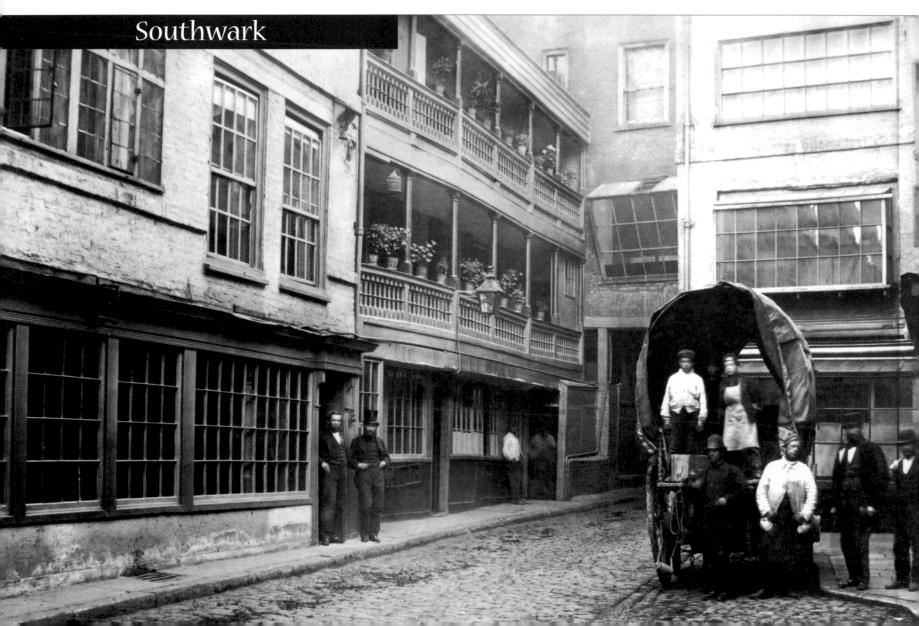

Southwark

Sutton

Top: SUTTON, THE COCK HOTEL 1890 27423A

Above: SUTTON, THE COCK HOTEL 1898 41708

The Cock Hotel, Sutton. Until the middle of the 18th century Sutton was a village focussed around The Green and the parish church, but of this phase little survives. The first catalyst for growth was the turnpiking of the London to Brighton road which went through Sutton from 1755 until 1809, when the route moved east through Croydon. Even so in the 1840s around twenty coaches a day changed horses at the Cock Hotel. An east-west turnpike road was laid out at the same time which ran from Epsom to Croydon and passed through Sutton, thus producing a major crossroads where development grew.

The Cock Hotel was built by the crossroads, and the superb first view (27423a) shows the old Cock Hotel in its 18th century state, complete with a Cycle Club badge and a hanging sign on a beam spanning the road, while to the left is the old beer-house, known as the Cock Hotel Tap. Eight years later (41708) the Cock Hotel Tap, demolished in 1896, has been replaced by a spanking modern hotel building in an ornate sub-Norman Shaw style with oriel windows, plaster friezes, a deep cornice and a steep roof with high dormers. The corner is emphasised by a lead-roofed turret and cupola. The old Georgian building behind was soon to be demolished, and its replacement itself disappeared in the redevelopment-crazed 1960s.

Croydon

CROYDON, THE SWAN AND SUGARLOAF HOTEL 1902   48181

The Swan and Sugarloaf Hotel, Croydon

The Swan and Sugarloaf has probably stood on this site since medieval times, but the present building is patently obviously, and indeed uninhibitedly, Victorian. Notice its symmetrical shape, the frivolous balcony at the front, the bow windows, the fake half-timbering, the ornate plasterwork, the lavish doorcases, and the finials on the gables. The pub stands in South Croydon at the junction of Brighton Road and Selsdon Road, a site with many historical links with transport. There was once a tollgate here; the horse trams from Croydon terminated here; in the 1880s the horse bus company stabled their horses here; and the motor buses had a bus stand here. But the electric trams (we can see one to the right of the pub in this photograph) ran past the Swan and Sugarloaf – their depot was further down the road.

From a bag of sugar to a tankard of ale

The pub's unusual name possibly derives from the coat of arms of the Archbishop of Canterbury, which has a mitre (shaped rather like an old-fashioned loaf of sugar) and a crosier (like a crook, in the shape of a swan's neck) – but this theory does seem rather tenuous. A more believable one is that the pub was originally the Swan, and also sold groceries; a sugarloaf was a common sign for a grocer's shop, so it originally displayed two signs, or combined the two symbols on one sign.

Upminster

The Bell, Upminster

East London expanded dramatically to embrace rural Essex in 1965 when the Greater London Council was created. However, London really is a series of villages and hamlets which have linked up. The further east you go, the more fine survivals of the former rural atmosphere will be found. Indeed, at the furthest Underground station, Upminster, the visitor will even find a windmill: Upminster's fine smock windmill in St Mary's Lane was built in 1804 and worked until as recently as 1934. It still stands in a field, and contains much original machinery which can be viewed.

The Bell, on the corner of Corbets Tey Road and St Mary's Lane, faced the churchyard. It was built in the 1770s by Sir James Esdaile, who embarked on improvements to the village at this time; there had been an earlier inn here, but set back from the road on the edge of the old village green. This quiet crossroads, with just James Matthews's coal merchant's cart stopped at the inn, would have been typical at the time, since Upminster was a quiet Essex town until the development of motor traffic. The spire of the National School peeps between the chestnut trees.

UPMINSTER, THE BELL 1908   60613T

The Bear Hotel, Maidenhead

By the mid 18th century Maidenhead was still much as it had been in medieval and Tudor times in terms of size: a single east-west main street running from the Smyth's Almshouses in the east to the foot of Castle Hill, then called Folly Hill, at the west. The street was lined with coaching inns such as the Sun, the Bear and the White Hart, with other inns including the Swan, and with shops and houses.

The original Bear Hotel was further up the High Street, near the present junction with Queen Street, on the south-east side of the former market place. Its landlord in 1489, John Fraunces, is mentioned in the Bray Manorial Court Rolls as 'charging an unlawful price for provisions'. The present hotel, its bear mascot's eyes glowing red, dates from the early 19th century. The wine merchant's premises belonging to J B Tyler at the time of this photograph (right) is now part of the Bear. To the left can be seen the tower of the now rebuilt parish church. The Bear was a busy coaching inn, serving the plenteous traffic along the Bath Road. Many people stopped at Maidenhead on their way westwards, because the Thicket nearby was frequented by highwaymen and thus not a pleasant area to travel through at night.

Maidenhead

Above: MAIDENHEAD, THE BEAR HOTEL 1890 23635

The Old George Hotel, Pangbourne

The Thames emerges from the Goring Gap at Pangbourne, and its valley widens out again. This photograph of Pangbourne was taken from the bridge over the Pang. The river rises on the Berkshire Downs, beginning as an intermittent chalk stream, or 'winterbourne', before maturing to a clear trout stream. Many varieties of plants grow in profusion along its banks. Pangbourne established itself as a popular haunt of artists, writers and weekend anglers. D H Lawrence and his wife rented a cottage in the village in 1919. The George's history goes back to the 17th century, and it was once a well-known coaching inn.

Pangbourne

Opposite right: PANGBOURNE, THE OLD GEORGE HOTEL 1899 42999   *Above:* PANGBOURNE, THE BRIDGE AND THE OLD GEORGE 1899 42998

Streatley

The Swan Hotel, Streatley

Now the Swan Diplomat Hotel, the main building is much extended to the right out of picture, to the left and to the front. The thatched room is now tiled, and the outbuilding to the left converted to hotel rooms. To the right is moored one of the Oxford College Barges. Jerome K Jerome described the river vistas around Streatley in his classic 'Three Men in a Boat' of 1889: 'Goring on the left bank and Streatley on the right are both or either charming places to stay at for a few days. The reaches down to Pangbourne woo one for a sunny sail or for a moonlight row, and the country round about is full of beauty. We had intended to push on to Wallingford that day, but the sweet smiling face of the river here lured us to linger for a while; and so we left our boat at the bridge, and went up into Streatley, and lunched at the Bull, much to Montmorency's satisfaction … It is an ancient place, Streatley, dating back, like most riverside towns and villages, to British and Saxon times. Goring is not nearly so pretty a little spot to stop at as Streatley, if you have your choice; but it is passing fair enough in its way, and is nearer the railway in case you want to slip off without paying your hotel bill.'

The joys of idling on the River Thames

J Ashby-Sterry perfectly expressed the joys of Victorian boating life in his 1886 verses:

'Yes! Here I am! I've drifted down –
The sun is hot, my face is brown –
Before the wind from Moulsford town,
So pleasantly and fleetly!
I know not what the time may be –
It must be half-past two or three –
And so I think I'll land and see,
Beside the Swan at Streatley!'

Above: STREATLEY, THE SWAN HOTEL 1899   42994

The Bull, Streatley

Downstream of Wallingford the Thames cuts the Goring Gap between the Chilterns and the Berkshire Downs. Brunel's Great Western Railway also took advantage of the gap for his route from Paddington to Bristol. One of the county's most picturesque villages, Streatley looks across the Thames to Goring, its Oxfordshire neighbour.

The Bull at Streatley stands beside a busy road junction, though it was a good deal quieter when these photographs were taken. The pub was once a coaching inn for the Royal Mail coach to Oxford.

Early in the 20th century, much of Streatley was owned by the famous Morrell brewing family. The main characters in Jerome K Jerome's 'Three Men in a Boat' visited the inn, which still boasts a post box and a water pump at the front.

The inside of this quaint old inn looks a little different today, but when this photograph was taken, the Bull epitomised traditional unspoiled country pubs. In those days, the saloon bar assumed the look of someone's cosy living room, with chairs arranged either side of the fireplace and bric-a-brac cluttering the walls.

Top: STREATLEY, THE BULL, THE SALOON BAR C1955 S221022

Above: STREATLEY, THE VILLAGE AND THE BULL 1904 52933

The Ostrich, Colnbrook

The Ostrich is said to be the third oldest inn in England. The present splendid timber-framed and jettied building dates from the 15th century, but it stands on the site of a far older one, perhaps of the 11th century. King John is said to have stopped here on his way to sign the Magna Carta in 1215.

A macabre murder story is attached to the Ostrich: at some time in the Middle Ages a Master and Mistress Jarman owned the inn. When a wealthy guest arrived, he or she would be allotted a special room where the bed stood on a trap door. As soon as the guest was asleep, the Jarmans would pull a hidden lever to release the trap door, and the guest would fall into a vat of boiling ale in the kitchen below. However, one morning the horse of a rich guest, Thomas Cole, was found wandering in the village; the Jarmans told an unconvincing story to account for Cole's disappearance, and when his body was found in the stream, they were arrested. At their trial they admitted to the murder of about 60 people, and were sentenced to be hanged. The stream's name, the Coln Brook, is said to derive from 'Cole in the brook'.

COLNBROOK, THE OSTRICH C1955   C494004

The George and Dragon, West Wycombe

West Wycombe escaped 1960s transformation. This is partly due to the Dashwoods, who conserved it until the National Trust acquired it in 1934. The village is a charming mix of timber-framed, brick, and flint buildings. West Wycombe played a key role in English furniture history as the location of the first recorded producer of the famous Windsor chair in 1732, and the beech woods hereabouts provided the raw material for furniture making, the main occupation here for centuries. In W340005 the photographer looks west past the red brick George and Dragon, a former 18th-century coaching inn on the Oxford road.

Chased through the Hell Fire caves

This inn is most famous for its ghost. Sukie was a servant at the inn in the 18th century. Her admirers were three village lads, but she wanted a better husband. She set about charming a rich guest at the inn, who was soon besotted; her humbler suitors were so jealous that they sent her a note, purporting to come from the rich young buck, suggesting elopement – she was to meet him in the notorious caves excavated by Sir Francis Dashwood to house the notorious Hell Fire Club. When Sukie arrived, her hidden suitors jumped out and chased her through the caves. Sukie tripped and fell, knocking her head. She was carried unconscious back to the George and Dragon, where she died. Two days later, the other maids who shared her room saw her ghost, and since then, dressed in white, she has haunted the inn.

Left: WEST WYCOMBE, THE GEORGE AND DRAGON C1955 W340005

The King's Arms Hotel, Amersham

Granted a market charter by King John in 1200, Amersham, only 26 miles from London, still has all the atmosphere of a venerable market town. Its High Street, lined by timber-framed and brick houses, is one of the best historic townscapes in Buckinghamshire – beyond the inn we can see a dignified Georgian house, and a short distance away is a 17th-century market hall. The King's Arms is one of the town's oldest coaching inns, but all is not as it seems in this photograph: all the timber-framing to the left of the RAC sign is modern, dating from 1936 when a plain Georgian block, itself tricked out with fake timber-framing, was drastically remodelled in the Tudor style using old timbers, with leaded casement windows and a jettied upper storey. Beyond, the older part of the inn is a genuine 16th-century hall house with jettied cross wings. Inside, much ancient oak flooring and beams remain, and beyond the old coach entrance is a mellow courtyard.

Election jollities

The King's Arms probably used to see much jollification at election time, according to J K Fowler in his 'Echoes of Old Country Life' (1892): 'The inns in Amersham were taken possession of at election time by the women folk, old and young, married and unmarried – the two best inns being selected by the lady inhabitants. Here the fair ones awaited the arrival of the newly elected members who formally entered the room and very deliberately and demurely kissed them in turns. This performance concluded, a raid was made into the inn by the young men of the place and amid loud laughter and screams and struggles innumerable they also kissed the not unwilling dames.'

Amersham

AMERSHAM, THE KING'S ARMS HOTEL C1955   A148072

The King's Head Hotel, Aylesbury

Aylesbury is a bustling country town. Its narrow streets are full of 17th- and 18th-century houses, and the County Hall in St Mary's Square dates from 1720. The church's spire dates from the 13th century, and the church has a 17th-century clock tower. The town was on a stagecoach route, and there are many very old coaching inns here, including the King's Head. This inn, one of Aylesbury's architectural treasures, is tucked away off the Market Square. It was given by the Rothschild family to the National Trust in 1926, and underwent major and scholarly restoration in the 1990s, but it is still run as a pub. The King's Head stands at the corner of the market square, which was surrounded by inns in medieval times; this particular inn is a rare survival. It was originally the guesthouse of a monastery, and became an inn in the 15th century. Beyond the arched passageway, wide enough to admit stagecoaches and carriages, is a large cobbled stable yard. The 20-light 15th-century window once lit the great hall (now the bar). Some original glass which dates from 1456 still survives, including armorial glass depicting angels bearing shields with the coat of arms of Prince Edward, killed at the battle of Tewkesbury, and of Henry VI and Margaret of Anjou who stayed at the inn whilst touring the country shortly after their marriage: a remarkable and rare survival amid the bustle of an inn through over five and a half centuries.

Aylesbury

AYLESBURY, THE OLD KING'S HEAD HOTEL 1921   70562

St Albans

ST ALBANS, YE OLD FIGHTING COCKS C1960   S2123

The Fighting Cocks, St Albans. There have been travellers passing up and down Watling Street, or the modern A5, to or through St Albans as long as time can record. This was the important Roman settlement of Verulamium, and the magnificent Norman tower of St Albans Cathedral is constructed with Roman masonry from the ancient city.

The Fighting Cocks, said to be the oldest inhabited licensed premises in the country, is a landmark among inns. Little changed today, it occupies the site of a monastery founded by King Offa in the 8th century. The building was built in the 11th century as an octagonal timber-framed dovecote; then it was a part of a fishing lodge attached to the monastery in pre-Reformation days. As its name implies, it was a cockpit from the 17th century until 1849, when cockfighting was banned. In the 17th century the inn played host to Oliver Cromwell and his troops as they passed through St Albans.

The Coopers Arms, Hitchin

The architecture fronting Hitchin's streets ranges from Tudor to Victorian. A good many of the buildings seem Georgian, but behind these façades there often lie earlier structures. Timber-framed houses were not always valued so much in the past as they are today, and new brick and stone frontages were frequently appended to earlier buildings. The Coopers Arms is a 15th-century building; the ground floor stone-mullioned windows incorporate some of the 15th-century tracery from the dismantled Tyler's Guildhall. The inn has a fine fireplace and interesting early cellars; there is reason to believe that the building was once much larger than it is today. In this photograph, McMullen's advertise their 'fine ales and invigorating stout'. The road surface shows signs of cobbling from an earlier age.

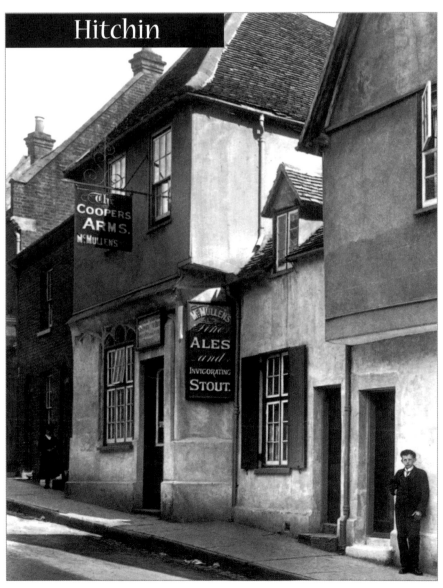

HITCHIN, THE COOPERS ARMS, TILEHOUSE STREET 1903   49745X

The Swan Inn, Elstow

Elstow is a small village about two miles south of Bedford. When John Bunyan walked the lanes and fields of Elstow in the 17th century, it was an isolated village a mile and a half south of the King's Ditch around that part of Bedford south of the River Ouse. Now Bedford's housing estates, business parks and industrial estates have swallowed the fields and have reached the north end of the village; they have spread east and west, but so far have not engulfed Elstow. However, Bunyan's birthplace was demolished in 1968.

Elstow

Above: ELSTOW, THE SWAN INN 1921 70452

The Swan Inn stands on the High Street, east of the church and the 16th-century Moot Hall. Most of the village was owned by the Whitbread family, including all the 16th-century timber-framed buildings in this photograph. Those on the left were sold to Bedford Borough Council for £1 in 1974 and restored: the roughcast was stripped and the timbers exposed. The Swan is still an inn and virtually unchanged today.

Along the Bunyan trail

John Bunyan, the son of a local brasier, and the author of 'The Pilgrim's Progress', was born at Elstow; he was christened in the Abbey Church of St Helena and St Mary in 1628, and lived in a small village cottage. Elstow has become a place of pilgrimage, and Bunyan's tribulations and his books are celebrated by the Bunyan Trail, a 75-mile-long footpath winding through the Bedfordshire countryside linking elements of Christian's journeys and Bunyan's life.

Henley-on-Thames

The Catherine Wheel, Henley-on-Thames

Henley is famous for its Royal Regatta, held during the first week in July. The first Henley Royal Regatta was held in June 1839 and it has been an important event in the town's social calendar ever since. Henley had become a busy coaching town by the 18th century, when several turnpike trusts transformed the road system to Henley's benefit: the Hurley Trust which improved the route from Henley to Maidenhead, the Reading and Hatfield Trust which passed through the town, and the Dorchester Road Trust from Henley to Oxford.

Many inns adapted to the new trade, including the Catherine Wheel (left of 31733), an inn established by 1499; here it is pictured before it had taken over the two Georgian town houses beyond – and when its name was spelt 'Catharine'. The coaching age brought a new lease of life to Henley – the town now catered for travellers from much further afield. The first regular coach service to London had been established in 1717. It ran from Henley's White Hart to the White Horse in Fleet Street, setting off at 6am and reaching its destination that evening, originally twice a week and returning 'with a good coach and six able horses perform'd (if God permit)'. With turnpike improvements the time for the journey reduced, so that at one time about twenty coach routes included Henley.

Above: HENLEY-ON-THAMES, THE CATHERINE WHEEL, HART STREET 1893   31733

RIGHT: HENLEY-ON-THAMES, THE REGATTA 1890   27201

Clifton Hampden

The Barley Mow Inn, Clifton Hampden

On the east bank of the Thames is the medieval Barley Mow Inn. Jerome K Jerome commends it in 'Three Men in a Boat' as 'the quaintest, most old-world inn on the river … a story book appearance while inside it is still more once-upon-a-timeyfied'. Jerome is said to have spent a lot of time watching the life of the River Thames from here, and it is claimed that he wrote much of his famous book at the Barley Mow. The building is noted for its cruck construction – note the large curved timbers in the gable wall. The timbers are now painted black rather than being (correctly) limewashed as in this view.

Opposite:
CLIFTON HAMPDEN,
THE BARLEY MOW
INN 1890   27010

Below:
CLIFTON HAMPDEN,
THE PLOUGH C1960
C121011

The Plough, Clifton Hampden

Jerome K Jerome described Clifton Hampden as a 'wonderfully pretty village, old-fashioned, peaceful, and dainty with flowers'. The old village consists of a number of small, picturesque thatched and timber-framed cottages to the west of the church and along a lane running west from the river bridge. On the north side of the road is the Plough Inn, a thatched building with late medieval cruck frames within.

The inn has been extended since this photograph was taken in the 1960s, but otherwise this view is relatively unchanged, although there is now a car park to the left.

This village was part of the estate of the Hampden family; John Hampden, Oliver Cromwell's cousin, was a prominent Parliamentarian politician, but soon after the Civil War began he was killed by Prince Rupert's cavalry. The Hampden Room in the Plough is named in his honour, and some have heard his ghost pacing the floor.

Broughton

The Saye and Sele Arms, Broughton

Broughton Castle, near Banbury in Oxfordshire, was built as a fortified manor house by Sir John de Broughton in the 14th century. It was later acquired by William of Wykeham, who converted the house into a castle. In the 15th century Broughton passed by marriage to the Fiennes family, and during the Elizabethan era the house was transformed into the Tudor building we see today. William Fiennes, 8th Baron Saye and Sele (nicknamed 'Old Subtlety' by Charles I), was a staunch Puritan, and played a leading role during the Civil War period; however, he hoped for a settlement with the king, and after Charles I's execution he retired from public life and spent much time on Lundy Island in the Bristol Channel, which he owned. Broughton is still owned by the Fiennes family, Lords Saye and Sele, today. The Saye and Sele Arms, which probably dates from the early 18th century, stands near the castle.

Left: BROUGHTON, THE SAYE AND SELE ARMS 1922 72116

William Shakespeare, travelling player

In medieval times, before theatres were built, travelling troupes of actors staged plays in inn courtyards; legend says that William Shakespeare once appeared in one of the many plays staged in the courtyard of the New Inn.

Left: GLOUCESTER, THE NEW INN C1950 G20048

Gloucester

GLOUCESTER, THE NEW INN 1912   65118

The New Inn, Gloucester. Abbot John Twining built the New Inn in 1455 (a replacement for the original one) for pilgrims to the shrine of Edward II at St Peter's Abbey. Then, as now, Gloucester was a populous, busy place, so gentlemen, yeomen, knights and dignitaries all came to the New Inn. Both of these photographs show the view looking from the inner courtyard through the passageway from Northgate Street at the front of the inn. This courtyard is the original medieval one with galleries running round the sides – it has been described as the finest example of a medieval galleried inn in Britain.

Lady Jane Grey was pronounced Queen of England whilst at the New Inn in 1553 – she was only 17 years old. Within months she was charged with treason and sentenced to death. A tennis court was built here in Tudor times. In the 18th century, showmen brought strange and rare marvels to the inn for the citizens of Gloucester to wonder at: Maria Theresa, the Corsican fairy (she was only 2ft 10ins tall), wax models of the royal family, a mermaid from Mexico ... As the years passed, the advent of coaches made the inn an important port of call for many travelling to London - the route did not change until motorways came in the 1960s.

Pembridge

PEMBRIDGE, THE NEW INN AND THE MARKET HALL C1955   P172019

The New Inn, Pembridge

Like so many New Inns, this one is actually very old, dating from the 1600s. There was an even earlier inn on this site, and here a treaty was signed in 1461 after the battle of Mortimer's Cross, a decisive battle in the Wars of the Roses, when the future Edward IV routed the Lancastrians. This wonderfully chequered inn is an outstanding example of timber framing, even in this region of black-and-white buildings. It was originally a farmhouse, and then was known for many years as the Inn without a Name – the farmer who built this house probably brewed ale, which he sold to the traders and sheep and cattle drovers at the market hall opposite. The inn also used to serve as the local courthouse.

The delightful market hall probably also dates from the 16th century; it was originally a two-storey structure, and it has been said that the upper floor was used as a lock-up for local miscreants, but this is generally thought to be unlikely. Beside it are two stones called nails, where deals were agreed or struck – hence the expression 'to pay on the nail'.

Twin haunting

Two ghosts haunt the inn, or so the locals say: one is visible only to women, and is a young girl awaiting the return of her lover from the war; no one knows if he is dead or if he has deserted her. The other ghost is a red-coated soldier wielding a sword and sometimes beating a drum, who tends to be seen haunting the gents' lavatory.

Pershore

The Angel Inn, Pershore

Pershore is an old market town of considerable charm on the right bank of the River Avon. Pershore's Fair began in the reign of Henry III to provide funds for the restoration of the presbytery; it was held in the churchyard until the mid 1800s. Merchants would come from right across the Vale of Evesham and the Cotswolds to sell their wares, and local villagers still make their way to Pershore for their shopping at least once a week. Since the dissolution of its abbey, Pershore has prospered from fruit growing. Its medieval bridge was badly damaged during the Civil War, but was soon restored to its former glory.

Much of the architecture of this country town is Georgian (though there are a few older buildings). In the 18th century the town became a staging post, and the Angel Inn, seen here, is an ancient posting inn, carefully restored a decade before this photograph was taken. Note the beautiful bow windows and the large arched entrance to the courtyard behind.

Left: PERSHORE, THE ANGEL INN 1931 84678

FRANCIS FRITH'S
CURIOUS PUB NAMES

Bucket of Blood
200 years ago the landlord was shocked at finding a man's head at the bottom of his well.

Round of Gras
From 'gras', a shortened version of asparagus, which is grown in the locality.

Pipe and Gannex
A pub at Huyton near Liverpool, the reference being to the pipe and Gannex raincoat worn by the former Prime Minister Harold Wilson, who was MP for the constituency.

Quiet Woman
Shows a woman carrying her own severed head, suggesting that women are only quiet after they're dead!

The Nobody Inn
Named after a former landlord of the pub at Doddiscombleigh who refused to open the door to customers.

Bag o' Nails
Possibly a corruption of Blackamoor's Head, or Bacchanals (drinking revels).

Babes in the Wood
The signboard shows two men in the stocks.

Bird in Hand
A hawking reference to the falcon on a gauntlet.

Cat and Bagpipes
Refers apparently to the Caterans, war-like Scots who carried out raids over the border to the village of East Harlsey.

Cat and Fiddle
Possibly Le Chat Fidele (the governor of Calais) or Catherine la Fidele (Catherine of Aragon).

The Why Not?
Refers not to the decision whether to take a drink or not, but to a Grand National winner at the end of the 19th century.

Alfriston

The Red Lion, Monkland

The man posing for the Frith photographer in front of the Red Lion is a postman in his uniform. The other people in the photograph are most probably customers at the pub, which makes one wonder how late in the day the postman was making his visit. Perhaps he was on his second (or even third) delivery round of the day. How times have changed!

A former vicar here, Sir Henry Baker, wrote many hymns and was a major compiler of 'Hymns Ancient and Modern'.

Left:
MONKLAND, THE RED LION INN 1906   55487

Droitwich

The Old Cock Inn, Droitwich

Droitwich developed as a spa in the early 19th century thanks to John Corbett, a local businessman, who opened the St Andrew's Brine Baths in the town for visitors. Not everyone came here for the waters – some visitors wanted something a little more intoxicating! The sign outside the Old Cock Inn in this photograph of Friar Street says: 'The Old Cock Inn, by Walter Harrison, licensed in the tenth year of the reign of Queen Anne. Retailer of foreign Wines and Spirits'. The 'tenth year of the reign of Queen Anne' was 1712.

At that time, and in this area of orchards, both cider and perry (made from apples and pears) would have been drunk, as well as ale. A strong drink called lambswool was often drunk here too – this was ale mixed with roast apple pulp, which made a lot of froth, hence the name. The Old Cock looks more like a church than a pub thanks to the window on the first floor, which came from the medieval church of St Nicholas in Friar Street. The church was pulled down in the 18th century, and the pub benefited from one of its windows.

Right: DROITWICH, THE OLD COCK INN C1910   D54003

The Royal Oak Hotel, Tenbury Wells

The River Teme rises in Wales and flows through Shropshire before entering Worcestershire at Tenbury. It lies at the centre of a countryside rich in small farms, orchards and market gardens, and Tenbury Wells is known even now as the 'town in the orchard'. Tenbury received its first charter for a market and fair in 1249, but remained a fairly humble country town until 1839 when a medicinal spring was discovered, leading to the creation of a pump room and spa, which was soon patronised by fashionable society.

One reason for Tenbury's success as a spa town was because it lay on the important coaching route between London and North Wales. The Royal Oak Hotel was a famous coaching stop, used by travellers who paused on their journey to take the waters. Its amazingly ornate frontage almost dazzles the eye; the half-timbered inn dates from the early 17th century. By the middle of the 20th century this old coaching inn had geared itself up to cater for motorised tourists; a later Frith picture shows it with antiquated leaded windows.

Below: TENBURY WELLS, THE ROYAL OAK HOTEL 1892   30849

Tenbury Wells

Ludlow

The Feathers Inn, Ludlow

With its castle and town established by the Normans at the end of the 11th century, Ludlow was later to become a most important military base controlling the Welsh Marches (or borders). In fact, by Tudor times the entire Welsh principality was being governed from Ludlow.

It is generally agreed by those outside the profession that lawyers charge too much. This large, grand and ornately ornamented house is the evidence. It was built by a lawyer, Rees Jones, in the early 1600s. In a period when just about every fine building in the county was owned by a wool or cloth merchant, this house reminds us of the importance of the legal profession to the wealth of Ludlow. By the end of the century it had become an inn with stabling for 100 horses. Today the decorative carving is much as it was when first built, with the exception of the balconies, which were added in the 19th century. The main room on the middle floor on the left has a truly magnificent plaster ceiling. The house is described by Nikolaus Pevsner as 'that prodigy of timber framed houses'.

The name of the hotel is derived from the ostrich feather carvings on the three gables; ostrich feathers are the badge of the Prince of Wales, and the house was built just after celebrations in 1616 at the investiture of the future Charles I as Prince of Wales. The Feathers remained an inn for the next 200 years, and was occasionally the scene of cock-fighting and prize-fighting. Candidates for parliamentary elections would make speeches from the hotel balcony, then invite voters inside for a drink to help secure their votes.

'Come you home of Monday
When Ludlow market hums ...'
Once this area was the entrance to Ludlow's market, with traders paying tolls at the nearby Tolsey (or toll booth), and refreshing themselves and striking their bargains over an ale in the Angel. The ashes of A E Housman, who wrote the above lines in 'A Shropshire Lad', are buried here in St Lawrence's churchyard in Ludlow.

Left: LUDLOW,
BROAD STREET AND THE ANGEL HOTEL 1936   87393T
Above right: LUDLOW,
THE FEATHERS HOTEL 1892   30829P

The Angel Hotel, Ludlow

Broad Street was described by Nikolaus Pevsner as 'one of the most memorable streets in England'. It is a wonderful mix of architectural styles, with 15th-century buildings at the top and elegant Georgian buildings further downhill, all overlooked by the tower of St Lawrence's Church, the largest parish church in Shropshire.

The Angel Hotel has recently been sold and refurbished as shops and apartments. It was built as an inn in 1555, and it is therefore older than the Feathers. Later it became a coaching inn, and among its most famous visitors were Admiral Nelson and Lord and Lady Hamilton, the latter being Nelson's mistress.

The Corbet Arms Hotel, Market Drayton. It was not only livestock, butter and cheese that were traded in the markets of Market Drayton. One especially famous market was held in the High Street every September – for the sale of damsons. These would have been picked locally, and were mainly sold to mill owners from Lancashire who used the damsons for dyeing cotton. In recent years modern chemicals have replaced natural dyes, and the Damson Fair is no longer held in Market Drayton, sad to say.

Just about every town in Shropshire has, or at least had, a Corbet Arms Hotel or pub. A powerful Shropshire family, the Corbets came over to England with William the Conqueror. We can only assume that the first Corbet was a man with black hair, because he was nicknamed 'the raven' ('corbiere' in Norman French), and his descendants have since used the raven as their crest. A raven can be seen carved on the Buttercross in Cheshire Street, and in the High Street the Corbet Arms Hotel clearly shows the raven on its signboard.

The building dates from the 18th century, and has been at the heart of town life ever since. Famous visitors to the Corbet Arms included Thomas Telford, who stayed here in 1832 when he came to inspect the canal which was then being built. When the railway age came, the hotel ran a special horse omnibus, the Station Omnibus, to meet all the trains. The carriage can be seen in this photograph, parked in front of the hotel (behind the Napier car).

A ghostly visitor to room seven

A permanent resident is the ghost that haunts Room 7. She was a young girl who was seduced and subsequently jilted by a hotel guest, and she committed suicide in this room. It is said that ever since then she appears when the room is occupied by a bachelor.

Above: MARKET DRAYTON, THE CORBET ARMS HOTEL 1911 63336

Bidford-on-Avon

The Old Falcon Inn, Bidford-on-Avon

Bidford-on-Avon is a large, attractive village six miles downstream from the town of Stratford-upon-Avon. It stands on the Icknield Way, a Roman road. The Falcon Inn in Bidford was once the scene of a drinking competition between William Shakespeare and his friends and a group of local lads known as the Bidford Sippers. The Stratford boys lost the bout and were too drunk to make the journey home, spending the night sleeping off the session under a crab-apple tree.

Shakespeare is said to have commemorated the drinking bout in a rhyme which satirises local villages: 'Piping Pepworth, Dancing Marston, Haunted Hillborough, Hungry Grafton, Dodging Exhall, Papist Wixford, Beggarly Broom, Drunken Bidford'; however, this rhyme was not printed until 1749 (in the Gentleman's Magazine), and is possibly not authentic.

Left: BIDFORD-ON-AVON, THE OLD FALCON INN 1901 47340

Edgehill

Left: EDGEHILL, THE CASTLE INN 1922 72072

The Castle Inn, Edgehill. The sounds of battle can be heard here, and a spectral soldier rides through the bar – for it was here in 1642 that the first major encounter of the Civil War took place. The battle of Edgehill was the first major battle of the Civil War, with the Parliamentarians led by the Earl of Essex and the Royalists by Charles I and Prince Rupert. It ended indecisively, and both sides claimed victory; subsequently Charles I felt confident enough to reject Parliament's offer of peace.

In 1742 Sanderson Miller, a local squire, began to build this octagonal folly, also known as the Radway Tower, and now the Castle Inn, to commemorate the 100th anniversary of the battle, and it was formally opened on 3 September 1750, the anniversary of the death of Oliver Cromwell. It is suitably warlike in character, for it does indeed look like a well-fortified castle. From the garden of the inn there is a wonderful view of the battlefield site between the villages of Radway and Kineton. Inside the inn is a collection of weapons found on the battlefield.

The horn dance

The Abbots Bromley Horn Dance ritual dates back at least as far as 1226 – it is first recorded as being performed at the three-day Barthelmy Fair in that year. However, it is believed to be much older than that, and has survived down the centuries, continuing to flourish today in this Staffordshire village.

The Goat's Head, Abbots Bromley

The fine timber-framed building to the left is the Goat's Head, which dates from the 17th century. It stands opposite a butter cross – this was once a market place, and the market was first recorded in the 14th century. This spot outside the inn is one of the many places in Abbots Bromley where the Horn Dance is performed every year. The original purpose of the dance is lost in the mists of time, although it has been suggested that it may have been a way of marking the parish boundaries, or 'beating the bounds'.

The horns themselves are 1,000 years old – they have been carbon dated – and the dance is performed on Wakes Monday. The horns are collected from the church in the morning, and carried aloft, the dancers performing their ritual to music played on a melodeon. The dancers – six Deer-men, a Fool, Hobby Horse, Bowman and Maid Marian – carry the horns around the village, stopping traffic and performing the dance many times. They trek up to ten miles, threading a path between the outlying farms and houses. Meanwhile, a jester strikes people in the crowd with a pig's bladder, which is said to encourage fertility.

Below: ABBOTS BROMLEY, THE HORN DANCE C1955 A165385

Abbots Bromley

Loggerheads

The Loggerheads Inn, Loggerheads

The phrase 'to be at loggerheads' means to quarrel or to resort to fisticuffs, and it was just a few miles along the present A53 at Blore Heath on 23 September 1459 that Yorkist and Lancastrian forces clashed for the first time since the battle of St Albans in May 1455. Was this the origin of the name of this 16th-century coaching inn? This pleasantly cottagey building, originally quite plain, has been given a Victorian facelift – big dormers with ornamental timbers and finials match the gable on the rustic porch. A party of ladies who lunch are awaiting their charabanc.

Left: LOGGERHEADS, THE LOGGERHEADS INN C1930 L432002

The Bell Inn, Finedon

The boot and shoe industry formed an important part of Northamptonshire's economy over a long period. Finedon, not far from Wellingborough, became a boot and shoe manufacturing village in the 19th century and expanded greatly at that time. Previously, it had been a small village with a market (it has had a market charter since at least 1294). There used also to be iron ore quarries here. In the older part of Finedon is the fine parish church, mostly 14th-century with an elegant recessed spire. The organ is said to have been played by Handel.

This part of the village is full of houses and cottages built by William Mackworth-Dolben, the Victorian lord of the manor. He built or altered many local buildings (including his own house, Finedon Hall, dating from Elizabethan times) in a somewhat eccentric mock Gothic style; none is more fanciful than the Bell Inn on Bell Hill. It was rebuilt, transforming an earlier, possibly 16th- or 17th-century building in 1872 – and apparently originates from 1042 as the Tingdene Hostelrie, a monastic hospice for travellers.

Finedon

FINEDON, THE BELL INN C1955 F184004

Oundle

OUNDLE, THE TALBOT HOTEL C1950   0103029

The Talbot Hotel, Oundle

Oundle is an attractive stone-built market town, situated in the north east of Northamptonshire with the River Nene flowing on three sides of it. It is home to the leading public school Oundle School, which was founded as a grammar school in 1556 by Sir William Laxton, a prosperous London grocer and Lord Mayor of London. The school remained modest in size until the mid 19th century, when it grew rapidly, and a large number of its fine stone buildings now dominate the north part of the town. Is that an Oundle boy crossing New Street with his arms full of books?

Opposite him is the Talbot Hotel, a very old inn, formerly the Tabret; it was largely rebuilt in stone in 1625. This stone came from Fotheringhay Castle, where Mary Queen of Scots was beheaded in 1587, and the inn's main staircase also came from the castle. It was down this stair that Mary came on her way to the block, and it is said that her ghost still descends this way. Mary's executioner stayed at the Talbot the night before he did his macabre duty.

Nottingham

The Flying Horse Hotel, Nottingham

Nottingham, famous for lace, cycles, Boots the Chemist, and Trent Bridge cricket ground, is also famous for its Goose Fair, which may have given this inn its name – a flying horse was a medieval roundabout, and the inn stands in the market place where the Goose Fair used to be held.

The building we see today dates from Elizabethan times, but its massive stone foundations are much older; it is known that in 1400 the site belonged to a medieval charity, the Plumtre Hospital. Below the ancient foundations are even more ancient caves and passages in two tiers, carved out of the sandstone on which Nottingham stands; how old these are, and why they were created, no-one knows for certain. This pleasant, rambling old inn, with its beamed ceilings and panelled walls, was for many years where the 'City Fathers' of Nottingham met – one room was known as the Mayor's Parlour. In the 18th century, it was the headquarters of the Tories during elections; in the 19th, it was frequented by the actors who performed in Nottingham's theatres.

NOTTINGHAM, THE FLYING HORSE HOTEL 1920   69427

NOTTINGHAM, YE OLDE TRIP TO JERUSALEM INN 1920 69430

Ye Olde Trip to Jerusalem, Nottingham

This ancient inn juts out of the rock – indeed, it is connected with the myriad sandstone caves just below Nottingham Castle, and cellars below the inn are carved out of the rock. As the sign outside the inn indicates, the building has been here from at least 1189. This was the year when Richard the Lionheart began the Third Crusade against the Saracens in the Holy Land, and legend has it that knights gathered here before their journey to Jerusalem – hence the inn's name. It is possible that the inn was originally the brewhouse for the castle – the brewing process requires a constant low temperature, which the caves provide; also, two 'chimneys' through the rock lead from the inn to the castle walls, which might have been used in the malting process, or to haul ale from the brewhouse up to the castle.

One of these chimneys leads from the Rock Lounge, a room carved out of the rock. Here guests can see the Cursed Galleon, a model of a ship that is said to bring death to anyone who cleans it – so it is shrouded with dust and cobwebs! Mortimer's Room, another rock room, is where Roger Mortimer and his lover Isabella, wife of Edward II, met – Mortimer was hanged for treasonously murdering the king. The parts of the inn outside the rock that we see today date from the middle of the 17th century, when it belonged to William Standford, a prominent citizen of the time.

The landlord who won't leave

Perhaps the most famous landlord at this Nottingham inn has been George Henry Ward, whose popular nickname was Yorkey – he was licensee from 1894 to his death in 1914. His ghost haunts the cellar caves, where he plays tricks on the inn staff by moving things around.

Saffron Walden

SAFFRON WALDEN, THE ROSE AND CROWN HOTEL 1932   85113

The Rose and Crown Hotel, Saffron Walden

Saffron Walden has been a market town since 1141. Dorothy Monteith writes that 'the first stalls were set up outside the south castle walls on the slope leading down towards the Cam. Gradually the houses were built to enclose a large rectangular market place … No cattle market is recorded by name, but cattle were sold in the open square. Animals continued to be sold in this manner until the new Cattle Market was constructed in the 19th century'.

The Town Hall (right) was enlarged in 1879 with a fine mock Tudor façade which bears the town crest. Barclays Bank (then Gibson & Son, left) was built in 1874. This is the only purpose built bank in the town, and like other banks still overlooks the commercial centre of the town – the market place. And where should everyone foregather on market days? At the Rose and Crown (next to Barclays), which had stood on that spot possibly since the 14th century. This was a wonderful old building with a decorative pargetted frontage put on in the 1880s. Alas, the building was gutted by fire in 1969. Later, when the frontage was demolished, the overportal was saved; it is now incorporated into a building behind, and the inn sign of a bunch of grapes now hangs outside Boots, which stands on the site – it must be the only chemist adorned thus.

Great Dunmow

The Dunmow Flitch

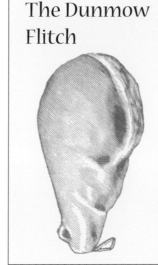

The Dunmow Flitch is an ancient custom whereby a flitch of bacon – a whole side of a pig – is presented to a married couple who can prove that they have not, in the past 366 days, 'offended each other in deed or in word' nor in any way regretted their marriage. If this sounds solemn, it was originally intended to. The process seems to have been instigated by the church as a means of underlining the sanctity of wedlock.

The Saracen's Head Hotel, Great Dunmow

Great Dunmow is justly proud of its Flitch, but it is important to remember that it is also a living, working town with its own long history. It developed from a Roman settlement at the intersection of two long, straight roads. Its market – granted in 1253 – was a busy conduit for the livestock, corn and dairy goods being produced by the area's farms. As with many other Essex towns, however, much of Dunmow's prosperity was to come with the influx of Flemish weavers at the end of the 16th century.

The Georgian façade of the Saracen's Head masks a 17th-century inn, but its name indicates that its origins go back to the days of the Crusades. Local tradition tells of an 18th-century landlord, well respected in the town, who led a double life: by night he was a highwayman, preying on the rich customers that he played host to during the day. This landlord was also a smuggler, and kept the cellars well stocked with contraband wine and brandy. The Saracen's Head was an important staging post in coaching days, and the stable yard, complete with the ostlers' tap room, still stands at the back. The inn has hosted numerous celebrations, meetings, balls and auctions at key points in Dunmow's history (such as the banquet to mark the coming of the railway). The annual parish dinners were held here in the 19th century. The flail, tun and wheatsheaf plastered on its façade represent the town's former sources of livelihood.

Top: GREAT DUNMOW, THE SARACEN'S HEAD C1955 D90002

Left: GREAT DUNMOW, THE FLITCH TRIALS, CHAIRING THE WINNERS 2000 D90705

Great Bentley

The Red Lion Inn, Great Bentley

This photograph gives an evocative view of a typical modest village inn. This one is the Red Lion, in this little village between Colchester and Clacton. Known for its huge village green, the largest in England, which covers some 42 acres (17 hectares), Great Bentley is still a place of quiet charm, little changed today. In its time, the green has seen tea-parties, dancing, football, cricket, flower-shows, horse-races and prize-fights. The village's steam mill was built in 1886, and lasted until 1925, when the chimney was demolished.

Left: GREAT BENTLEY, THE RED LION INN 1902 48290P

Braintree

The Horn Hotel, Braintree

This photograph (46241x) shows the Horn Hotel, a fine 17th-century coaching inn with cobbled courtyard. It provided nourishment for the farmers driving hard bargains in the Corn Exchange two doors away. Pigot's Directory of 1824 stated that the Norwich Day coach called at the Horn at 10am and 4pm (at this time the journey from Braintree to London took five hours).

In the 17th century the area in front of the hotel was used as the meeting place for the weekly market and the annual fair, and cattle and horses were still being sold in the High Street in the later years of the 19th century. This area was also the setting for a famous 1826 print of people attending Braintree Market; in 1979 the local Chamber of Trade commissioned a painting depicting members of the local community standing in the same place. The Horn continued to serve the community until 1970. It was then closed, and shops were put in on either side of the carriageway, which retains its cobbled entrance.

BRAINTREE, THE HORN HOTEL 1900 46241X

COLCHESTER, THE RED LION HOTEL C1960   C136038

Colchester

The Red Lion Hotel, Colchester

The Red Lion's story begins 2,000 years ago, when Colchester was the Roman town of Camulodunum: it stands on the site of a luxurious Roman house, and two fine mosaic floors have been found here. The next oldest feature of the inn is a 14th-century stone doorway in the vaulted cellars, traditionally monastic in origin. Part of the building we see in this photograph (C136038) – the two bays to the right of the main entrance – dates from about 1470, when it was built as a two-storey hall house. Very soon afterwards, the building was greatly enlarged and turned into an inn. This is a masterpiece of 15th-century carved woodwork inside and out. Both the upper stories are jettied, and the huge oak gateway leads to a cobbled courtyard. The rear yard, also jettied, now leads to the Lion Walk shopping mall.

The Red Lion is reputed to have two ghosts, one of a young girl who haunts the kitchen, and the other of a monk who died in a fire.

Woodbridge

The Crown Hotel, Woodbridge

'Woodbridge at high water he has approached by the same fairway as the adventurers and traders of the Middle Ages, ... an old-world fairway, that is now as then it was. This is a spot that is very England.'

So wrote the 1930s writer Alker Tripp in his 'Suffolk Sea-Borders', and the sailing fraternity would agree today that the only way to approach the town is up the River Deben. Its history and character and its spirit are closely bound to that river. From the Middle Ages to the 17th century, ships were built here for the Royal Navy. The photograph shows a traffic conductor, one of a small fraternity who assumed this role following the birth of the motor car, helping pedestrians outside the Crown Hotel.

It may not look it, but the Crown is very old; there are ancient foundations and beams in the cellars, and some remnants of half-timbering from the 16th century. Much of the interior has 18th-century panelling. Ancient manorial courts were held here from medieval times to the 19th century. A 17th-century landlord was Peter Pett, the shipwright who built the ship that brought Charles II home from exile in Holland in 1660. Early in the 19th century the Prince Regent, later George IV, was a regular customer at the Crown; he was passing through on his way to the Marquis of Hertford's estate at Sudbourne, where the attractions were the hunting and the delightful Lady Hertford.

WOODBRIDGE, THE CROWN HOTEL C1955   W128017

Felixstowe

The Ferry Boat Inn, Felixstowe Ferry

Felixstowe was developed as a seaside resort by Colonel George Tomline in the 1870s. He built houses for residents and visitors, encouraged the railway to bring in tourists, and created docks and harbours to bring trade and employment. After the three-week visit of the German empress in 1891, Felixstowe became known as 'the Queen of the East Coast Resorts'. The town was built around a wide shingle bay which offered excellent safe bathing. Sir Cuthbert Quilter established a steam-powered chain ferry between Felixstowe and Bawdsey. The two ferry boats, commissioned in 1894, were the 'Lady Quilter' and the 'Lady Beatrice'; they operated until 1931.

In this photograph at Felixstowe Ferry, just north of Felixstowe, we can just see a cart making a delivery to Margaret Rogers, landlady of the Ferry Boat Inn at this time, while in the foreground children make daisy chains and play with a toy cart. The inn was built in the 17th century, and has now been extended and modernised. It stands near the harbour and the Martello tower between the dunes and Felixstowe Ferry golf course, the setting of M R James's famous ghost story, 'Whistle, and I'll Come to You, My Lad', one of the most frightening stories ever written.

Above: FELIXSTOWE, THE FERRY BOAT INN 1907 58990

Ipswich

The Great White Horse Hotel, Ipswich

Ipswich, seated at the head of the Orwell Estuary, has been a major port for centuries, and thus a destination for travellers, who need rest and refreshment. In these photographs we are looking west along appropriately-named Tavern Street (with Cornhill in the distance and the Town Hall clock tower). On the right-hand side is the unassuming Georgian façade of the Great White Horse Hotel, which actually hides a much older timber-framed 16th-century building.

Famous guests at the hotel included George II in 1736, Louis XVIII of France in 1807, and Lord Nelson, who in 1800 was High Steward of Ipswich. By the 1950s (I18036), the Great White Horse Hotel has acquired stone cladding, several signs, and a set of traffic lights. How strange it is that the buildings on the left look more authentically old than they did in 1893! These seemingly Tudor façades are in fact reproductions, built in the 1930s when such imitations were in vogue.

Left: IPSWICH, THE GREAT WHITE HORSE 1893 32202

Below: IPSWICH, THE GREAT WHITE HORSE C1955 I18036

Mr Pickwick and the curling papers

In its time the Great White Horse Hotel has played host to the prolific Victorian novelist Charles Dickens (above), who wrote about the inn in 'The Pickwick Papers' – it was here that Mr Pickwick returned to the wrong room and disturbed a lady wearing yellow curling papers.

FRAMLINGHAM, THE CROWN HOTEL, MARKET HILL C1955 F45005

Framlingham

The Crown Hotel, Framlingham. Although best known for its castle, Framlingham's heart is Market Hill, where many of the buildings are in fact made from stones removed from the castle, which was pulled down in the 17th century. However, its outer walls remain, enclosing a large space, which in the 18th century was used for prize fights. In 1744, for instance, John Slack, the Norfolk pugilist, defeated John Smith, the Suffolk champion not once, but twice; a vast crowd of boxing enthusiasts from all over the country came to see the fights.

No doubt many of that crowd visited the Crown, which at that time was enjoying its heyday as a coaching inn – the large central passageway leads into a picturesque courtyard with stables beyond. According to 'Tales of Old Inns' (2nd ed 1929), a door in the passageway leads to a 'graceful and really fine staircase, of early 18th-century date at the latest. This sweeps in broad shallow steps up to the first floor, its carved balusters and handrail suggesting immediately the age of hoops and of bewigged gallants, so many of whom must have passed up and down this fine staircase. For the staircase leads direct to the doors of a handsome chamber, at one time the Assembly Room of Framlingham, the scene of numberless routs and balls and feastings in times gone by.'

Long Melford

LONG MELFORD, THE BULL HOTEL C1955 L101002

The Bull Hotel, Long Melford

This area in the south-west of Suffolk is famous for its so-called wool villages and churches, including Lavenham, Long Melford, Sudbury, Monks Eleigh and Chelsworth. However, it was not sheep farming which gave rise to the region's immense wealth in the Middle Ages, but the organised production and export of woollen cloth; the term 'dyed in the wool' comes from the local practice of dying the yarn before it was woven into cloth.

The splendid timber-framed Bull Hotel dates from c1450, when it was built for a wealthy cloth merchant, and has been an inn since at least 1580. The impressive façade was uncovered in 1935, when a Georgian brick frontage was removed. Inside is a finely carved wall post inscribed 'AED 49', probably the initials of a Mr Drew, the landlord in 1649, who refurbished the inn then. The inn is said to be haunted by the ghost of a yeoman murdered in the 17th century.

The woodwose, wild man of the woods

In one room at the Bull there is a carving of a woodwose. 'Tales of Old Inns' (2nd ed 1929) tells us that 'woodwoses, or wild men of the woods, were very popular subjects among medieval sculptors in this part of England; you will often find them around the bases of fonts in Suffolk churches. The woodwose of the Bull is naked, save for a wreath of foliage around his hair and a similar girdle around his loins. He clasps a huge club in one hand, and the other, outstretched, holds the neck of a swan-like bird, apparently flying down into its nest, which may be seen close to the wild man's right foot. What tale he has to tell you must surmise for yourself.'

King's Lynn

KING'S LYNN, THE HONEST LAWYER INN 1925 78717

The Honest Lawyer Inn, King's Lynn

King's Lynn has a significant history of brewing, and it was considered at one time to have had many pubs of poor reputation. In 1892 the King's Lynn Vigilance Committee (a temperance group) reported that there was one licensed house for every 100 inhabitants, man, woman or child – indeed, in Lynn at that time one house in 23 was licensed. The licensing act of 1902 tidied things up, although the landlord at the time this photograph was taken, Elliott or Edward Lofts, was fined 10s in 1914 for selling alcohol to a boy who was not yet 14 years old. The Honest Lawyer, situated at the corner of London Road and Southgate Street, was believed to have been named after a lawyer who in fact was thoroughly dishonest: after a long career of crime, he was eventually executed for smuggling.

St Ives, Overcote

The Pike and Eel Inn, St Ives, Overcote

St Ives parish, which includes Overcote, is rich in attractive old buildings. It stretches along the north bank of the River Great Ouse, where the 300-year-old Pike and Eel Inn stands at Overcote Ferry.

This classic inn interior calls up former days. The floor is brick, with a rush mat on top, and there is plenty of well-polished furniture, while a fine 8-day country-style long case clock (probably made c1800) ticks patiently in the corner. Knick-knacks and various ornaments are displayed round the walls and on the mantelshelf, including a grinning Toby jug, candlesticks, and calendars, and a mirror hangs on the wall beside the clock. Note how dark this room is – it has tiny windows and no electric light. The chief feature of the room, of course, is the fireplace; it was originally a huge inglenook fireplace, but at some point a central hearth has been raised and enclosed with bricks and cement and whitewashed. A salt box hangs to the right of the fireplace. The bellows will soon set the logs in the hearth ablaze, and we can sit down by the fire and enjoy the hot toddy waiting on the table.

Left: ST IVES, OVERCOTE 1914 66973

Above: ST IVES, OVERCOTE FERRY, THE PIKE AND EEL INN, THE FIRESIDE INTERIOR 1914 66976

Buckden

The Lion Hotel, Buckden

Buckden in the county of Cambridgeshire is mentioned in Domesday; its name derives from 'buccadenn', 'valley of the he-goats'. It was probably in the 12th century that the bishops of Lincoln built a palace here, though the remains visible today date from about 1490. Buckden, now bypassed but originally situated on the Great North Road, had two coaching inns facing each other, the Lion Hotel and the George Inn.

The Lion Hotel, once the Old Lion and Lamb, was famous as a coaching inn in the 18th and 19th centuries, but its history goes further back than that. It may well have been the refectory of the bishops' palace, for in what was the old kitchen the beautiful moulded 15th-century ceiling rafters meet at a magnificent oak boss carved with a lamb and flag and the words 'Ecce Agnus Dei' ('Behold the Lamb of God'). The original building of c1500 was timber-framed and jettied. In later years the Lion absorbed the buildings on either side of it.

Above: BUCKDEN, THE LION HOTEL, HIGH STREET C1950   B237001

The Ferry Boat Inn, Holywell

Holywell is situated in fenland country not far from Ely. Its holy well is said to cure blindness – and tradition says that Boudicca and her Iceni tribe used it. The Ferry Boat Inn, on the banks of the River Great Ouse, is one of the oldest inns in England; it is said that there was an alehouse here in the 10th century, but the oldest part of the inn as it stands today is 600 years old. There is a large inglenook hearth where a fire is always kept burning, ancient oak beams, and a terrace overlooking the river – the Ouse can flood in the winter, and rises up to the height of the walls. The Ferry Boat is a favourite haunt of fishermen.

The ferry which gave the inn its name (66971) operated until the 1930s; it was pulled by a chain across the river. Villagers took the ferry to go to work in Over or to cycle to Cambridge. The reeds on the bank of the river were harvested for rush matting by the Arnold family – the rushes were dried hanging over lines beside the river. The reeds were used in wickerwork and basket making.

Holywell

Jilted Juliet

Ghost-hunters come here in the hope of seeing the ghost of Juliet Tewsley, who died in the 9th century. Jilted by her lover, a woodcutter called Tom Zoul, she committed suicide on St Patrick's Day (17 March), and was buried on the bank of the river near the ferry, now the site of the inn – her gravestone can be seen in the bar. From here her ghost is said to float towards the river every St Patrick's Day.

Top: HOLYWELL, THE FERRY BOAT INN C1960 H407060   *Above:* HOLYWELL, THE FERRY AND THE FERRY BOAT INN 1914 66971

Grantham

The Angel and Royal Hotel, Grantham

Grantham's medieval wealth was based on wool from the sheep grazing the Kesteven fields. Later an industrial town, it retains much of its Georgian and Victorian brick rebuilding of what had been a stone town. It stands on the Great North Road, the main south-north route since medieval times, and the Angel and Royal, one of the most remarkable of medieval inns, has been a stopping-place for over 750 years. Its history begins when it belonged to the Knights Templar; it was an important enough hostel for King John and his court to stay here in 1213. But the earliest part of the building that survives today is the main archway, carved with the heads of Edward III and Queen Philippa.

The rest of the noble stone frontage dates from the 15th century; the grand upper room is known as the Chambre du Roi, or the King's Room, and it was here in 1483 that Richard III heard of the treachery of the Duke of Buckingham and signed his death warrant. In the ground floor rooms is some beautiful fan vaulting over the bay windows, one with a carving of a pelican feeding her young with her own blood. Much later, in coaching days the Angel became one of the busiest inns on the Great North Road, and hundreds of coaches stopped here. The archway leads to a large stable yard, flanked by long wings added in the 18th century.

A landlord's sobering bequest

One of the many interesting stories about the inn concerns Michael Soloman, the landlord, who died in 1706. In his will he left 40 shillings to be paid each Michaelmas Day for the preaching of a sermon against drunkenness – this custom endures to this day.

Left: GRANTHAM, THE ANGEL AND ROYAL HOTEL 1893 33257

Above: GRANTHAM, THE ANGEL AND ROYAL HOTEL 1893 33258

Far right:
STAMFORD, THE
GEORGE HOTEL
1922 72305

Above:
STAMFORD, THE
GEORGE HOTEL,
THE COURT-
YARD 1922
72321B

Near right:
STAMFORD,
THE GEORGE
HOTEL, THE
DINING ROOM
1922 72321C

The George Hotel, Stamford. Stamford, one of England's most attractive and historic towns, is only just in Lincolnshire. Much of 18th-century Stamford's trade came from its location on the Great North Road, and it had numerous coaching inns. The George is probably the best known, an inn since 1568 and noted for its famous sign spanning High Street St Martin's, which provides a memorable entrance to Stamford from the south. The 1920s motorist appears well catered for in photograph 72305, with both garaging and petrol to hand. The days of flood lighting have arrived too, although at this time the lights are illuminating the George's sign rather than the front of the building as they do today. Note the old fashioned AA sign on the wall of the hotel. The courtyard is still walled with ivy, although it is not today used for parking cars.

Stamford

Left: CHESTER, BRIDGE STREET, THE OLD KING'S HEAD 1888 20600

Opposite: CHESTER, YE OLDE BLUE BELL 1929 82757

The Old King's Head and Ye Olde Blue Bell, Chester

The King's Head stands on the west side of Lower Bridge Street, a few minutes' walk downhill from the Cross. The pub's name refers to Charles I's stay at nearby Gamul House during the Civil War. This splendid inn, described as a 'new building' in 1633, was once the home of Randle Holme I, Mayor of Chester in 1633–34. Four generations of the Holme family were heralds and historians in Chester in the 1600s.

Ye Olde Blue Bell and its companion, Ye Olde Cabin, have been trading from the 15th century – 'Licensed 1494', proclaims the painted sign on the near gable. Both establishments are not bashful about telling the passer-by what they provide. It was off to the pub for a pint of mild, best mild, or best bitter, and to the Cabin, which calls itself a 'soda fountain bar', for ices and iced drinks in summer and hot drinks (Bovril or Oxo) in winter.

In fact, this is the oldest building in Chester, and the city's only remaining medieval inn; parts of the building date from the 11th century, and the construction of the timber roof dates it to between 1250 and 1400. The inn's name may refer to the abbey curfew bell, rung in the abbey bell-yard nearby every evening in medieval times, and the abbey had a brewhouse, which could have supplied the inn. The licensee at the time this picture was taken was the wonderfully-named Thomas Pogmore Tushingham. Soon afterwards, in 1930 the city council bought the inn for £1,000 so as to demolish it for road widening. Local people strongly protested and the inn was saved, only for it to be threatened again in 1960. Again, the objections of locals saved it; today it is an oriental restaurant.

Chester

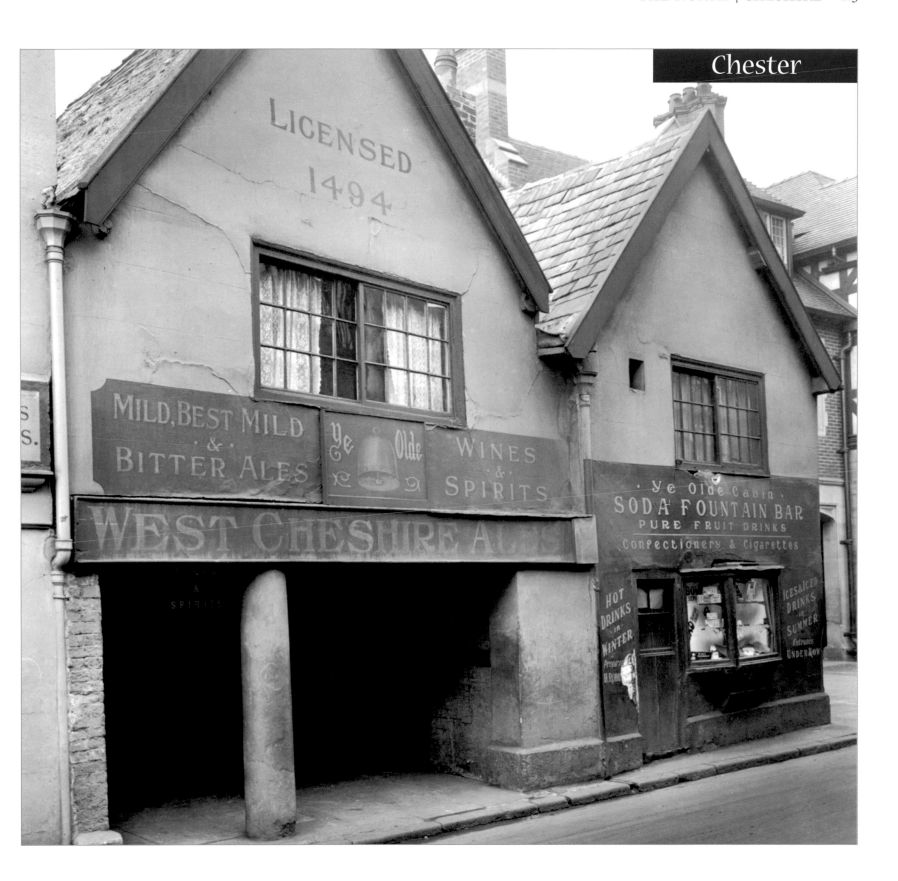

Knutsford

KNUTSFORD, THE ROSE AND CROWN 1898 42119

The Rose and Crown, Knutsford

The people of Knutsford will tell you that this town's name comes about because there was a ford here for King Canute. Knutsford was home for many years to the writer Elizabeth Gaskell. She taught at the local Unitarian chapel Sunday School, and she and her husband William are buried in the chapel yard. Mrs Gaskell became a very close friend of Charlotte Brontë and wrote her biography. Her novel 'Cranford', published in 1853, gives a delightful picture of town life in mid 19th-century England. The original Rose and Crown, probably dating from the 1600s, is the gabled part to the right; the much later brick extension on the left has been given the black and white treatment – fake timber framing has been painted on!

Among the famous patrons of the Green Man at Ashbourne in the 18th century were James Boswell and Dr Johnson; they did not in fact stay here, but they were given a meal by the landlady Mrs Killingley when they visited the town.

'I took my post-chaise from the Green Man, a very good inn at Ashbourne, the Mistress of which, a mighty civil gentlewoman, curtseying very low, presented me with an engraving of the sign of her house; to which she had sojoined in her own handwriting, an address in such singular simplicity of style that I have preserved it, pasted upon one of the boards of my original journal at this time, and shall here insert it for the amusement of my readers. "M Killingley's duty waits upon Mr Boswell; is exceedingly obliged to him for this favour, whinever he comes this way, hopes for a continuance of the same. Would Mr Boswell name the house to his extensive acquaintance. It would be a singular favour conferred on one who has it not in her power to make any other return but her most grateful thanks and sincere prayers for his happiness in time and in a blessed eternity."'

JAMES BOSWELL

Ashbourne

The Green Man and Black's Head Inn, Ashbourne. The inn sign in St John Street is a rare example of a 'gallows' sign, extending across the road. The inn may have the longest name in the world: 'The Royal Green Man and Blackamoor's Head Commercial and Family Hotel' – it is 'royal' because Queen Victoria, when a princess, stopped for tea.

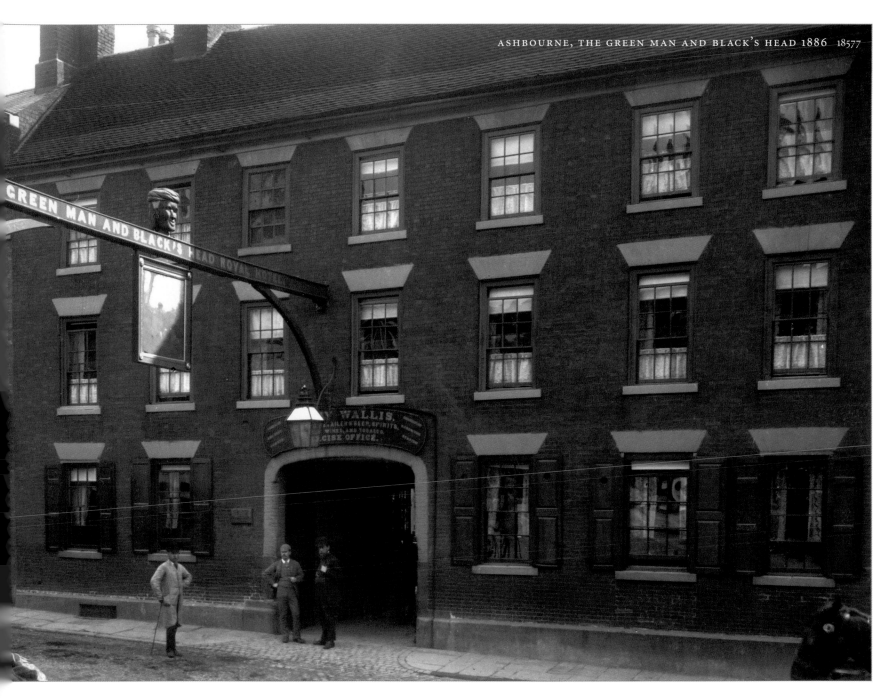

ASHBOURNE, THE GREEN MAN AND BLACK'S HEAD 1886 18577

The carved blackamoor's head at the centre of the sign has two faces – it smiles at those entering Ashbourne, and scowls at those who leave! The present inn was built in 1750, and is actually two separate inns joined together. Note the cobbled street – and is it an ostler from the inn's stables standing beneath the sign?

The name of the Green Man goes back to medieval times, or even earlier; the green man was the main figure in May Day celebrations – he was killed and then brought back to life, to the joy of the May Queen. He was probably originally a pagan nature god, but he is nonetheless a common subject for medieval church carvings. Near the Green Man was the Blackamoor's Head (usually shortened to the Black's Head). One of the town's main inns, it was once used for important events and as the local law courts – in 1748 the County Assizes were held here. During the Napoleonic Wars it was known as the Holyoak Hotel, and a French priest held services here for French prisoners of war. At the beginning of the 19th century the landlord of the Green Man bought it and joined the two inns on one site.

Rowsley

ROWSLEY, THE PEACOCK INN 1886 18617

The Peacock Inn, Rowsley

The bridge over the River Derwent at Rowsley, about four miles north of Matlock, was built in the early 17th century and still carries today's busy traffic on the A6 trunk road. The mellow gritstone walls of the Peacock Hotel are a landmark to visitors coming into the Peak District from the south. The inn dates from the mid 17th century, and was originally the grand, beautiful house built by a certain John Stevenson – he specified fine mullioned windows with diamond-paned glass, a large, castellated porch with a room over the entrance, and ornate chimneys. The house was sold to the Manners family, the Dukes of Rutland at nearby Haddon Hall. They used it as their Dower House and then as a farmhouse, and eventually in 1820 it became an inn. The peacock crest of the Manners family can be seen over the porch.

The Cat and Fiddle, Buxton

This remote pub on the Buxton to Macclesfield road was popular with Victorian visitors on a trip out from Buxton, and remains popular today, particularly among motorcyclists, who congregate there at weekends, though their motorcycles look considerably different from the specimen in 67581 – note its wicker sidecar. Although it has been expanded in recent years, the pub is still surrounded by miles of inhospitable moorland. It has been known for the pub to be cut off for days during heavy snowfalls. The Cat and Fiddle was, and still is, the highest public house in England with a full licence – it stands on Axe Edge, 1,707ft above sea level, sturdily built in sombre local stone to withstand wind and weather. Down the years it has proved a welcome haven for travellers overtaken by nightfall in these bleak surroundings. It is said that inns called the Cat and Fiddle get their name from Catherine la Fidele, 'faithful Catherine', probably Catherine of Aragon, first wife of Henry VIII.

Buxton

Top: BUXTON, THE CAT AND FIDDLE 1914   67582   *Above:* BUXTON, THE CAT AND FIDDLE 1914   67581

OLD WHITTINGTON, THE REVOLUTION HOUSE 1902   48902

The Old Cock and Pynot, Old Whittington

The cottage in the foreground is the Revolution House, formerly the Cock and Pynot Inn (a pynot is a local name for a magpie), in the village of Old Whittington, north of Chesterfield. This was where three local noblemen met in 1688 – they were the Earl of Devonshire (from nearby Chatsworth), the Earl of Danby and Mr John d'Arcy. They were discussing the ways and means of achieving the Glorious Revolution of 1688, which brought about the removal of the Catholic James II from the throne and his replacement by his Protestant daughter Mary and her husband William of Orange, who became the joint sovereigns William and Mary in 1689. The old Cock and Pynot is now a museum, and the present-day Cock and Magpie stands behind it, as it did in 1902.

FRANCIS FRITH'S CURIOUS PUB NAMES

Duck and Acid Drop
Slang name for the Swan and Sugarloaf.

George and Cannon
A corruption of the name of George Canning, the 18th-century Prime Minister.

Turk's Head
Either a reference to a local rope industry (a Turk's Head is a kind of knot), or to the Crusades, when many inn names had references to Turks or Saracens.

Goat and Compasses
Said to derive from 'God encompasseth us'.

Goose and Gridiron
Slang for the Swan and Harp.

The Frighted Horse
Originally the Freighted Horse (a pack horse), but the 'e' has been dropped.

Muddy Duck
Slang for the Black Swan.

Naked Man
Reference to the biblical Adam.

The Ostrich
From Ostry (Hospitalaria), a monastic guest house.

Swan with Two Necks
A swan with two nicks (marks on his bill).

Duke Without a Head
Originally the Duke's Head, but at some time in the past the landlord applied to transfer his licence to a different building. The reply came from the authority: 'Permission is given to remove the Duke's Head'. And so the landlord did.

Bull and Spectacles
Once the Bull's Head, but renamed many years ago after an inebriated customer climbed up the wall of the pub and put his spectacles on the head of the bull.

Manchester

The Seven Stars Inn, **Manchester**. The sign on the Seven Stars Inn proclaims it to be 'the Oldest Licensed House in Great Britain, licensed over 540 years'. This is very hard to prove, as early licenses were issued very haphazardly, and for different reasons. It was said that this old inn had many tunnels radiating from its cellars, and that Guy Fawkes once hid in them. Unfortunately, this lovely old building was pulled down and cleared away as recently as the 1930s.

Below: MANCHESTER, THE SEVEN STARS INN C1900 M21301

Middleton

Ye Olde Boar's Head, Middleton

Middleton is an ancient place, its name suggesting a Saxon origin. And, with such a history, it is heartening to know that some of its very old buildings still survive. One is this 16th-century inn which stands on the corner of Long Street. Half-timbered and built upon a stone plinth, it was apparently once used as the courtroom and jail. According to legend, a secret tunnel leads from the cellars of this inn to the parish church.

Residents who were born in Middleton can lay claim to the traditional title of 'Moonraker'. Poachers, surprised by the sudden arrival of the local constable, tossed their catch down in the waters of a pond and began raking at the reflection of the moon which was shining below. When interrogated, they said innocently that they were trying to rake in the great yellow cheese.

Above: MIDDLETON, YE OLDE BOAR'S HEAD C1955 M311502

Gandhi in Clitheroe

Gandhi stayed at the Swan & Royal in 1933 when he visited Mrs Garnett's cotton mill at Low Moor in 1933. So impressed was he with the mill, that he adopted some of the ideas in use at Clitheroe for the cotton industry in India.

The Swan and Royal Hotel, Clitheroe

'A township, parochial chapelry, market town, corporate and parliamentary borough', was how Clitheroe was described in 1840.

CLITHEROE, THE SWAN AND ROYAL 1921   71130

Clitheroe

The Honour of Clitheroe, held in medieval times by the de Lacy family, comprised the parishes of Blackburn, Chipping, Ribchester, Bury, Rochdale and the Forest of Bowland; its 28,800 acres were all controlled and run from Clitheroe Castle. The Charter of Incorporation for Clitheroe was granted in 1147, making it the second oldest town in Lancashire. Castle Street is Clitheroe's main shopping street. We are outside the Swan & Royal. The sign seems to say it all: a garage is provided for the modern motor car, bait for those who come for the fishing, and stables for the horses. The hotel was originally the Swan; it was visited by the travel writer John Byng, who in 1792 reported that his bedroom door was broken and everyone could see him in bed. Apart from the castle, this is the highest part of Clitheroe, 300ft above sea level. It is here that the morris and folk dancing takes place once a year at the Clitheroe Folk Festival, an event not to be missed.

Barrowford

BARROWFORD, THE WHITE BEAR INN 1950 B302028

The White Bear Inn, Barrowford

On Thursday 20 August 1612, three generations of so-called witches were marched through the crowded streets of Lancaster to a gallows on the moor one mile away. The clergyman in attendance intoned 'God show them mercy', but in their wretched lives they had been shown none. Poverty was perhaps their only crime; the charge of witchcraft was exacerbated by their accusers' ignorance and malice. This execution was the culmination of a long-standing feud between two families that ended in the destruction of each other.

ALBRECHT DÜRER'S
'FOUR WITCHES' 1497

The women were brought down by a mistaken belief in their own powers of black magic and by false testimony; but also the rare opportunity to be noticed and to have attention paid to them was irresistible, unaware as they were of James I's new draconian laws against witchcraft. The fascinated interest in their fate and in the unexplained mysteries shrouding the event is as strong today as it was 500 years ago.

Barrowford is where the Pendle Witches Trail begins. The 45-mile route takes visitors through historic villages and on to Lancaster Castle via the Trough of Bowland.

This famous coaching inn is situated in that part of Barrowford which stretches along Gisburn Road, where many interesting old properties stand; it was built originally as the great house of the Hargreaves family, and it is the largest 17th-century building in the village. The datestone reads 1607, but 1697 is a more accurate date: the original datestone was misread owing to weathering when rebuilding of the inn took place in 1912. When John Hargreaves died in 1713, an inventory of his house was made room by room, from the milk house to the great parlour. The building has been an inn since 1775; the name no doubt refers to the cruel practice of bear baiting, a common entertainment in these days.

Above: ELDWICK,
DICK HUDSON'S PUB 1921
71288

Eldwick

Dick Hudson's Pub, Eldwick. The attractive village of Eldwick is situated near Bingley in West Yorkshire. Dick Hudson's pub was originally called the Fleece – Dick Hudson was the landlord long ago. The pub is a popular watering hole for walkers en route from Shipley Glen to Ilkley by way of Rombald's Moor (named after a legendary giant, Rombald, who is said to have lived on that bleak spot). In Shipley Glen is the Shipley Glen Tramway; this funicular cable-hauled tramway travels up and down the glen, which is a sea of blue at bluebell time.

Bolton Abbey

The Devonshire Arms Hotel, Bolton Abbey

The majestic ruins of Bolton Priory, built in the 12th century, have been a popular attraction for painters, including Turner and Landseer, for many years, and also for tourists. The priory was home to 26 canons of the Augustinian order (known as Black Canons because of the colour of their habits). At the Dissolution of the Monasteries in 1539, the 13th-century nave of the priory church was saved to become the parish church.

The Devonshire Arms Hotel at Bolton Bridge is less than a mile from the ruined priory. At the time of photograph 61883, the 40-bed hotel was already a favourite with motorists, although the hotel had a carriage for hire for guests arriving by train. Originally a coaching inn, the Devonshire Arms stands in the Bolton Abbey Estate, which has belonged to the Dukes of Devonshire since 1733; the hotel contains paintings and antiques on loan from the Duke of Devonshire's seat at Chatsworth. The estate is situated in the Yorkshire Dales, so the hotel is set in the midst of some spectacular scenery, with 80 miles of trails and footpaths, including ancient woodland and moorland, and 7 miles of walking beside the beautiful River Wharfe.

Above: BOLTON ABBEY, THE DEVONSHIRE ARMS HOTEL 1909 61883

Haworth

The Black Bull Hotel, Haworth

Haworth is a small town of cobbled streets and plain grey stone houses set amidst the moors near Keighley. It is a place of literary pilgrimage, for in the parsonage here lived the Brontë sisters, Emily, Charlotte and Anne, and their brother Branwell. Their father was the vicar of St Michael and All Angels' Church. The moors around were beautiful but bleak, and the sisters led often solitary lives. The wild landscapes surely gave them the inspiration for their novels.

As for Branwell, he spent much time here at the Black Bull; despite being an alcoholic and an opium addict, he was very good company, and the landlord would often send for him to entertain visitors to the inn. However, in 1845 his consumption of drink and drugs killed him; his sister Emily, weakened by tuberculosis, caught a cold at his funeral and died ten days later. Haworth was a mill town, and the smoke from the mill chimneys stained the stone walls of the Black Bull, which stands at the top of the steep main street.

The Brontë chair of writing

A footpath leads out of Haworth to Lower Laithe Reservoir, the beautiful Brontë Falls, the Brontë Bridge (H194036), and the Brontë Stone Chair – here, tradition has it, the sisters took turns to sit and write. The path continues up on the moors to Top Withens, now a ruin, which is said to be the original of Heathcliff's farmstead in Emily Brontë's 'Wuthering Heights'.

Above left: HAWORTH, THE BLACK BULL HOTEL C1955 H194024
Below left: HAWORTH, BRONTË BRIDGE C1955 H194036

Hardraw

The Green Dragon, Hardraw

At the southern end of the Buttertubs Pass, Hardraw is located just a mile outside the market town of Hawes. Hardraw's name derives from the Old English, and means 'shepherd's dwelling'; this area once belonged to Jervaulx Abbey in Wensleydale, whose monks were famed for their vast sheep farms.

The Green Dragon is a very old inn, with parts of the building dating from the 14th century, and a priest's hole was found during alteration work in the 1970s. Other parts of the inn date from the Georgian era. The Green Dragon's grounds stretch along Hardraw Beck and the spectacular gorge of Hardraw Scar, the rocky amphitheatre of Hardraw Force, at 100ft England's highest waterfall.

A disastrous flood

The rock in these parts is limestone, a porous rock through which rainwater flows very quickly, causing rivers to rise dramatically if there is heavy rainfall. In 1889 there was a disastrous flood when a wall of water crashed over Hardraw Force and destroyed many houses, and even washed coffins and tombstones from the graveyard. The Green Dragon was badly damaged – the water roared in at the back and out again at the front, taking the furniture with it and smashing the beer barrels.

Right: HARDRAW, THE BAR PARLOUR, THE GREEN DRAGON C1955 H208024

The Rose and Crown Hotel, Bainbridge

The houses and cottages of Bainbridge nestle around the wide village green, shaded by old trees and overlooked by a Roman settlement. Nearby is the River Bain, the shortest in England, and Semerwater, the largest lake in Yorkshire. Bainbridge was once the 'capital' of Upper Wensleydale. The whitewashed façade of the Rose and Crown Hotel, one of Yorkshire's oldest inns (it dates from the 15th century), is a landmark on the main road through Wensleydale. It is often referred to as 'the Pride of Wensleydale'.

Above: BAINBRIDGE, THE GREEN AND THE ROSE AND CROWN 1896 38292

Below: BAINBRIDGE, THE ROSE AND CROWN C1960 B5010

An ancient custom is still carried out here today: every evening, from the Feast of the Holy Rood (27 September) to Shrove Tuesday in spring, a huge horn, which hangs in the hotel, is brought outside, and three long notes are blown. This tradition dates from Norman times, when Wensleydale was covered in dense forests, and Bainbridge was a safe haven for the foresters (and for travellers and drovers too). Every evening the horn blower would sound the horn to guide them all down from the lonely fells at dusk.

Bainbridge

West Witton

The Heifer, West Witton

West Witton, which stands at the eastern entrance to Wensleydale, lies in the shadow of Pen Hill on the southern side of the dale. It was a lead-mining village until the mid 19th-century. Coaches and carriages would pass through West Witton on their way to Aysgarth.

The Heifer (called the Wensleydale Heifer today) is a 17th-century coaching inn (63453), still complete with stables and mounting block at the rear; it is still open for travellers, although today it is more a restaurant with accommodation than an inn. Opposite was the old Library and Reading Room, which was later used as additional accommodation for the Heifer Inn. A few years ago the horse trainer Ferdy Murphy bought this annexe for use by his visiting jockeys. In August every year the village celebrates the age-old custom of the Burning of Bartle, a thief who stole sheep from the monks of Jervaulx Abbey and was burned at the stake.

Top: WEST WITTON, THE HEIFER INN 1911 63453

Above: WEST WITTON, THE VILLAGE 1911 63451

KNARESBOROUGH, THE MOTHER SHIPTON INN 1914   67264

The Mother Shipton Inn, Knaresborough

Knaresborough stands above the River Nidd on a sandstone cliff, and it is said that Mother Shipton was born in a cave here in the 15th century. She was renowned as a prophetess; she wrote her prophecies in verse, and among other things foretold Sir Walter Raleigh's discovery of tobacco and potatoes in America:

> 'From whence he shall bring
> A herb and a root
> That all men shall suit,
> And please both the ploughman and king'.

The Mother Shipton Inn, which stands in front of her cave, was originally a 17th-century farmhouse. The Dropping Well is a petrifying well, similar to those at Matlock Bath in Derbyshire, where the limestone content of the spring water solidifies objects which are placed in it. At one time the star attraction here was a petrified mongoose!

Newby Bridge

The Swan Hotel, Newby Bridge

Newby Bridge, spanning the River Leven, is the highest bridging point before Lake Windermere. The five-arched bridge dates from the 17th century and formed part of the turnpike route from Kendal to Ulverston. There are pedestrian bays on each pillar to help those on foot dodge the traffic.

The hotel stands on the north bank of the River Leven, by the bridge. From the earliest medieval times, this has been a place where travellers received hospitality, firstly from the monks of Furness Abbey, who farmed the lands hereabouts, and provided shelter for travellers at their farmhouses; they also collected tolls from travellers on busy routes or river crossings, and they are thought to have controlled the old stepping stones near the hotel. The oldest part of the Swan dates from 1623, when it was built as a farmhouse and alehouse not long after the first (wooden) bridge was built; the stone bridge we see today was built in 1651–52.

In 1763, the turnpike road from Kendal through Newby Bridge to Ulverston was constructed, and the Swan became a busy coaching inn – it was a stopping point for the Royal Mail coaches too. It was at this time that the Swan's grand Georgian frontage was built. Thanks to the boats and the coaches, the Swan remained a prosperous inn throughout the 19th century, while the neighbourhood remained prosperous too, thanks to the gunpowder and ultramarine blue pigment industries. Today, the Swan is much extended, and caters for the tourists who flock to this beautiful area.

> *For centuries pig-iron had been produced in the area – iron ore was mined hereabouts, and charcoal for smelting came from the forests all around – and in the 18th century, boats unloaded their cargo of charcoal at the landing stage at the Swan.*

Left: NEWBY BRIDGE, THE SWAN HOTEL 1914 67414P

Borrowdale

The Borrowdale Hotel, Borrowdale

This is one of the wildest valleys of Lakeland. Early visitors to the Lake District were horrified at the expanses of naked rock and seemingly threatening mountains of places like Borrowdale, and feared to travel far into the dale, until the Lake Poets, led by William Wordsworth, led the public to see the beauty of the Lakeland landscape and popularised the picturesque mountain scenery. Then the tourists began to come to the area, to Wordsworth's dismay – see his comments on the right. The Borrowdale Hotel was one of the first buildings here to be erected solely for the use of visitors. Built in 1866 at the foot of Shepherd's Cragg, it stands near the southern end of Derwentwater, where the River Derwent flows out of Borrowdale into the lake. To the north is Keswick. The hotel has been refurbished in Victorian style, complete with the original 41 room bells.

Above: BORROWDALE, THE BORROWDALE HOTEL 1895   36947

Wordsworth, in his 'Guide to the Lakes' of 1810, expresses his doubts as to the beneficial effects of grand scenery on ordinary people. He felt passionately that 'a vivid perception of romantic scenery is neither inherent in mankind, nor a necessary consequence of even a comprehensive education'. It was hardly surprising, therefore, that he felt a growing resentment at the invasion of his beloved fells by the increasing number of visitors staying at hotels such as the one shown here in Borrowdale. A true appreciation of the Lakeland scenery, Wordsworth believed, was only possible for those of the most refined sensibilities.

'There is not, I believe, a single English traveller whose published writings would disprove the assertion, that, where precipitous rocks and mountains are mentioned at all, they are spoken of as objects of dislike and fear, and not of admiration. Even Gray himself, describing in his journal, the steeps at the entrance of Borrowdale, expresses his terror in the language of Dante: "Let us not speak of them, but look and pass on".'

The Fish Hotel, Buttermere. This hotel stands in one of the Lake District's most beautiful valleys, five minutes' walk from Buttermere Lake and Crummock Water and at the foot of Honister Pass; it is one of the oldest inns of Lakeland. It became renowned as a centre for good trout fishing, and after the Lake Poets had made the beauty of the area known, tourists began to flock here.

In the 1790s, the inn was run by a family named Robinson. The innkeeper's daughter Mary was about 15 years old when a certain Joseph Palmer stayed at the inn in 1792. He later wrote one of the very first guidebooks, 'A Fortnight's Ramble in the Lake District', in which he described 'the Maid of Buttermere': 'Her hair was thick and long, of a dark brown, unadorned with ringlets, and did not seem to want them. Her face was a fine oval, with full eyes and lips as red as vermilion. Her cheeks had more of the lily than the rose.' This brought Mary some fame – tourists came to see her, and she was mentioned in other guidebooks – but she was destined for greater fame still.

In 1802 a gentleman claiming to be the well-born Colonel Alexander Hope stayed at the inn and quickly wooed and won Mary – they were married in October. Thanks to Mary's fame, the event was reported (by the poet Samuel Taylor Coleridge!) to the London papers, who found out that Mary's husband was actually an imposter named John Hatfield; he turned out to be already married – and a bankrupt. He fled to Wales, but he was arrested by the Bow Street Runners and sent to Carlisle to be tried for bigamy and false pretences – found guilty, he was hanged. These tragic events brought Mary national fame for a while. She eventually married Richard Harrison of Caldbeck, who helped her to run the Fish Hotel.

Buttermere

BUTTERMERE, THE FISH HOTEL C1873 6805

Ambleside

The White Lion and the Royal Oak Hotels, Ambleside

Ambleside stands at the northern end of Windermere. It has a long history – from medieval times it has been a centre for copper mining, slate quarrying, farming, charcoal burning, and the cloth trade, and it once had thriving corn and bobbin mills on the River Rothay. After William Wordsworth and the other Lake Poets made the wild, romantic scenery of the Lake District popular, Ambleside became a busy tourist town. In this photograph (left) we are in the centre of Ambleside; a coach and four has pulled up in the market place outside the White Lion, and the bustle in the main street shows how busy Ambleside had become as a tourist centre by the early 20th century.

AMBLESIDE, THE WHITE LION AND ROYAL OAK HOTELS 1912   64303

Greta Bridge

Left: GRETA BRIDGE, THE MORRITT ARMS HOTEL 1933 G103307

Top: GRETA BRIDGE, THE MORRITT ARMS HOTEL, THE BAR C1955 G103027

Above: GRETA BRIDGE, THE MORRITT ARMS HOTEL, THE BAR C1955 G103037

The Morritt Arms Hotel, Greta Bridge

The stone-built Morritt Arms, which stands on the banks of the River Greta, is located on the site of a Roman settlement – this was one of the main routes to Scotland from ancient times. The building we see today dates from the 17th century; there was a farm here then, and some of the farm buildings were converted into the inn.

In coaching days, this was an important stopping place – a fact which the proprietors exploited in the bar murals celebrating Dickensian characters and the excitement and romance of the time. These murals were created in 1946 by Jack Gilroy, a portrait and landscape artist, in just eleven days; the faces of some of the Dickensian characters are said to be portraits of local people.

The inn has many associations with artists and writers, who were perhaps inspired by its beautiful location; Charles Dickens, for instance, along with Hablot Browne, who illustrated his books, stayed here in 1839 on their way to Barnard Castle (Dickens was researching 'Nicholas Nickleby' – in this novel, Nicholas meets Wackford Squeers at Greta Bridge). The painter John Cotman stayed here too – his atmospheric watercolour of the old bridge dates from his visit – and so did Joseph Turner; he painted Rokeby House, the home of Squire Morritt, who gave his name to the inn. Sir Walter Scott wrote about the area too, including Rokeby House and Brignall Banks.

At the end of the coaching era, the Morritt Arms survived by adding a garage and petrol station to the inn. A ballroom was added in 1930.

Blanchland

Top: BLANCHLAND, THE SQUARE C1955   B555078

Above: BLANCHLAND, THE LORD CREWE ARMS FROM THE CHURCHYARD C1935   B555040

The Lord Crewe Arms, Blanchland

The charming village of Blanchland is situated in a narrow, deep, green vale on the north side of the Derwent, nine miles from Hexham. Its name is derived from Norman French, and means 'the white lands' – this could refer to the white habits of the monks of the Premonstratensian abbey that was founded here in 1165. After the Dissolution in 1539, the abbey buildings were converted into houses.

The Blanchland estate eventually passed into the hands of Lord Crewe, Bishop of Durham, and on his death to the Lord Crewe Trustees, who in 1752 began the restoration and repair of the by now dilapidated village. Thus Blanchland became in effect an 18th-century model village, built on the plan of the monastic buildings and out of their old stone. The houses and the Lord Crewe Arms (B555078, left) are grouped round what was the cloister of the abbey and its second courtyard (where there was a silver refinery and a fulling mill, possibly belonging to the abbey), all built out of what remained of the abbey buildings.

In the centre of the village is the famous Lord Crewe Arms. Some of this building was originally part of the abbey buildings (the abbot's lodgings, the guest house and the abbey kitchens) and dates from the 12th century, and some of the building was remodelled in the 17th century.

The ghost of Dorothy Forster, sister to Tom Forster who led the doomed Jacobite uprising in 1715, is said to haunt the inn to this day; apparently she asks guests at the inn to take a message to her brother, who had fled to France. It was he and his sister who sold the village to Lord Crewe, Bishop of Durham.

The Rose and Crown, Tintern. The abbey at Tintern has long been a place of beauty and fascination to visitors. Founded in 1131, it was the first Cistercian monastery in Wales. Like so many other abbeys, it suffered during the Dissolution, and only ruins remained. It was not until the 18th century that Tintern began to attract the tourist. Men were employed to clear away two centuries of debris to reveal the buildings, if not in their former glory, at least in picturesque dilapidation.

Visits by the artist Joseph Turner, who sketched the abbey and later produced some wonderful watercolours of the site, and the poet William Wordsworth (who of his poem 'Lines Composed a Few Miles Above Tintern Abbey' said 'No poem of mine was composed under circumstances more pleasant for me to remember than this') did much to promote the area, and visitors flocked to the abbey.

In the 19th century a new road past the abbey was built, and visitors continued to come to Tintern – and to need refreshment at inns like the Rose and Crown. This inn was built around 1835 in the centre of the village on the banks of the River Wye. The sign under the tree on the right in photograph 76881 advertises the hotel as recommended by the Cycle Touring Club. Today, the ivy has been removed and the walls whitewashed.

Tintern

TINTERN, THE ROSE AND CROWN 1925 76881

Abergavenny

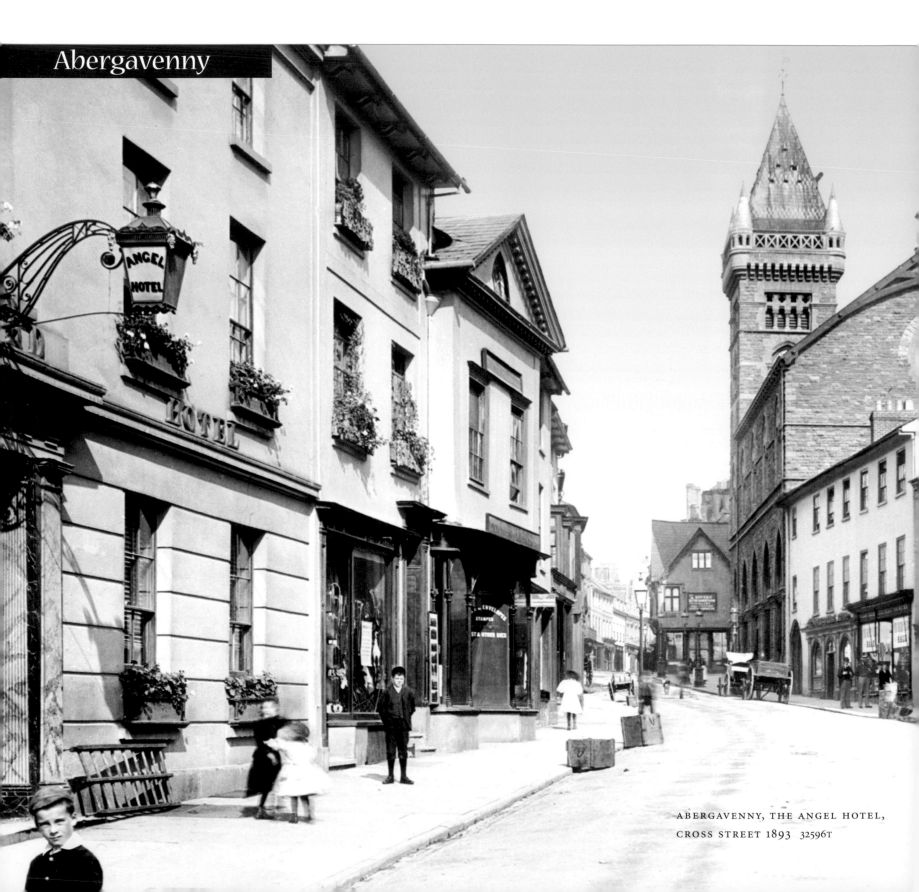

ABERGAVENNY, THE ANGEL HOTEL,
CROSS STREET 1893   32596T

RAGLAN, THE BEAUFORT ARMS HOTEL 1914 67685x

The Angel Hotel, Abergavenny

Nestling between the Black Mountains and the Brecon Beacons, and near the beautiful Usk valley, Abergavenny is about half-way between London and Milford Haven, and has long been a stopping place on the road; the Angel is a fine early Georgian building, refurbished in coaching days, when it gained its dignified façade.

The inn was busy in the coaching era. The coach from London to Milford Haven, the 'Champion', took 15 hours to reach Abergavenny, a difficult, gruelling journey, and its passengers were happy to receive all the hospitality the Angel could provide. The Royal Mail coach stopped here too. After 1858 the London service ceased, but the daily coach from Ross-on-Wye still stopped here.

Hollywood meets Wales

Famous people associated with the Angel include the ironmaster Crawshay Bailey, who attended a fancy dress ball here in 1838; Walter Morgan, whose family lived here, who was Lord Mayor of London in 1905; Gregory Peck the film star, who stopped here in 1945 on his way to film 'Moby Dick', heavily bearded for his role as Captain Ahab; and Richard Burton and Elizabeth Taylor in 1963, who consumed steak and kidney pie and a bottle of claret.

The Beaufort Arms Hotel, Raglan

This inn hides a long history behind its 19th-century façade. In 1646, during the Civil War, Fairfax's Parliamentatian soldiers sat drinking here during the three-month siege of Raglan Castle. Later in its life, in coaching days, the inn was an important stop on the South Wales route to Fishguard, from where boats plied to the Irish ports. The nearby Wye and Usk rivers are renowned for the good fishing to be had there, and the inn has accommodated several famous fishing enthusiasts, including a Prime Minister or two. There are said to be secret passages running beneath the inn, one leading to the parish church opposite.

Raglan Castle is probably one of the most majestic castles in Wales. Set upon a ridge amidst a wonderful landscape, it has cast an impressive shadow over the area for centuries. Raglan was at its height during the Elizabethan period, when the poet Thomas Churchyard visited in 1587, and wrote:

> 'Not farre from thence, a famous Castle fine,
> That Raglan hight, stands moted almost round:
> Made of freestone, upright as straight as line,
> Whose workmanship in beautie doth abound.
> The curious knots, wrought all with edged toole,
> The stately Tower, that looks ore pond and poole:
> The Fountain trim, that runs both day and night,
> Doth Yeeld in showe, a rare and noble sight.'

Parkmill

The Gower Hotel, Parkmill

The beautiful Gower Peninsula in South Wales was the UK's first designated Area of Outstanding Natural Beauty; it is an unspoilt region of downland, moor, and dramatic coastline. Parkmill is an old settlement. Here it is still possible to see the earth bank or pale, with a wall and inside ditch, which marks the boundary of the medieval deer park known as Parc le Breos.

The Gower Hotel was a popular coaching inn – a traveller in 1861 wrote: 'The resting place is a neat and pleasant inn, the Gower Inn, where good sitting and sleeping rooms may be obtained.' In the past rents were collected here, and in the 21st century, the inn is still popular. The attractive building in the centre is the former school, now the West Glamorgan Guides Activity Centre.

PARKMILL, THE GOWER HOTEL 1910   62589

Tregaron

The Sunny Hill Hotel, Tregaron

Tregaron was a small town, which grew rapidly during the early 19th century when it became a popular meeting place for drovers. The Abergwesyn pass leads through the mountains to the east of Tregaron. Along this road, thousands of cattle with 'cues' or two-part iron shoes, and sheep, pigs and geese, the latter with their feet dipped in tar and sand, walked to the Welsh border and beyond, where they were fattened ready for sale to English markets. This route was chosen because it had no expensive toll gates. The railway took this trade away after it arrived in 1866.

After this, although flocks of sheep and herds of cattle no longer congregated at Tregaron ready for the walk to England, the town continued to serve as a market place for livestock for many years. Ffair Caron was held for three days in March, while there were sheep fairs in June and September and hiring fairs in November. Here, farmers smartly dressed in three-piece suits follow one of the flocks to market. The hotel, in Station Road, is still in business.

Left: TREGARON, THE SUNNY HILL HOTEL, MARKET DAY 1933   T187005

Griffiths' Temperance Hotel, Tenby

It may seem a contradiction in terms to include a temperance hotel in a book about inns, but the temperance movement was a huge influence on 19th-century society. Indeed, it has been estimated that by 1900 about a tenth of the adult population were total abstainers from alcohol – and if they were away from home, they needed somewhere free from temptation where they could stay. The temperance movement began in 1832, when Joseph Livesey and seven Preston working men signed a pledge that they would never again drink alcohol. By 1835 the British Association for the Promotion of Temperance was formed. Its influence grew until in some parts of Britain public houses were forced to close on Sundays, and permission was rarely granted to allow new ones to open. Lady Rosalind Carlisle (1845–1922), a prominent temperance campaigner, used her influence to close down pubs or convert them into temperance hotels or coffee houses.

Tenby, a fishing and trading port from ancient times, and a medieval walled town, had become a seaside resort in the 19th century thanks to Sir William Paxton, a wealthy London banker, who recognised the potential of Tenby with its magnificent cliff-top setting. Fine, elegant terraces were built, together with hotels and lodging houses. Tenby was now a popular resort for the wealthy. This photograph shows Quay Hill in the old part of the town leading down to the harbour. The guests at Griffiths' Temperance Hotel may not be having anything very exciting to drink, but they will have a feast of seafood for their supper – note the basket loaded with shellfish and an enormous flatfish.

Left: TENBY, GRIFFITHS' TEMPERANCE HOTEL 1890   28076

Crickhowell

The Dragon Hotel, Crickhowell

Crickhowell is most famous for its grand 17th-century bridge over the Usk; Table Mountain is nearby. In recent years it has become a busy base from which to venture out onto the Brecon Beacons, either on foot or by car. The absence of motor cars and the un-tarmaced road in this photograph makes the town look much more tranquil than it does now.

This pleasing old inn first opened for business in 1740. Its licensee at the time of the Frith photograph was Elizabeth Davies – her signboard has been squeezed awkwardly between the two first-floor windows. The window on the left is in the beautiful Venetian style, multi-paned and with a rounded arch. Simple and unfussy, it adds elegance to an otherwise plain exterior.

Outside the hotel, to the far right, stands a row of watering cans on a sheet of corrugated iron, which is balanced between two barrels. Farther along are more barrels and boxes. Could this be one of Elizabeth Davies's sidelines? A little further along, outside the next-door lower building, now a private residence, is a display of garden spades. Note the fine lamp post on the other side of the road with the Post Office name painted on the glass. Today the lamp post has gone, but a modern, larger lamp in a similar style is attached to the wall of Carlton House (number 25). The ivy-clad house on the right, Latham House, retains its railings but has lost the ivy.

Left: CRICKHOWELL, HIGH STREET AND THE DRAGON HOTEL 1898 41695

Welshpool

The Mermaid Inn, Welshpool

Lying in the valley of the Severn, this ancient market town three miles from the English border does not seem particularly Welsh. Its original name was 'Pool', with the 'Welsh' prefix added to distinguish it from Poole in Dorset. The Victorian town hall and its dominating clock tower overlook some fine Tudor and Jacobean town houses.

Welshpool has had an anxious history, situated on the border with England, and has been destroyed on several occasions. As if to emphasise this, a small timber-framed inn stands neatly between later, or modified, buildings. The inn, formerly the Black Boy, dates from the 16th century, but the front elevation is part of the restoration of 1890 by Frank Shayler, an architect from Shrewsbury who specialised in vernacular revival work. The building used to be thatched, and the timber framing was originally plainer, and rendered over. One of the rooms has a fine ceiling divided into panels by beams, and at the back of the inn is a long wing, also timber-framed.

Left: WELSHPOOL, THE MERMAID INN C1955 W471011

Tynycornel Inn and Hotel, Tal-y-Llyn

In translation, Tal-y-Llyn means 'the end of the lake', which aptly describes the location of the village, with its little church and inns in the shadow of Cadair Idris. It sits at the south-western end of the lake, where the River Dysynni comes tumbling out in a series of little cascades. The lake has always been famous for trout fishing. This view of Tal-y-Llyn lake – Llyn Mwyngil in Welsh – looks much the same today, with the slopes of Cadair Idris rising up on the left. On the right-hand shore the B4405 snakes along towards Cross Foxes and Dolgellau.

In 1844 the late Colonel Vaughan of Hengwrt, the owner of the lake, built a small hotel. This was the Tynycornel Inn and Hotel, and the good Colonel provided boats for his guests. An angler named John Henry Cliffe wrote the following in 1860, and his description of the view from the inn can hardly be improved upon: 'Nothing in landscape can exceed the soft beauty of the Tal-y-Llyn; under peculiar lights – especially after rain or in lowering weather – the exquisite sight of the mountains on either side is perfectly magical. The contrast from the sublime to the beautiful leave an impression upon you which time cannot erase.' Today the building has been extensively refurbished, but care has been taken to ensure that all the 15 rooms have a lakeside view.

Tal-y-Llyn

TAL-Y-LLYN C1965 T2087

Bala

BALA, THE WHITE LION HOTEL 1913 65847

The White Lion Hotel, Bala

The medieval borough and market town of Bala is situated in a rural part of Meirionnydd. This spacious town's elegant main street is lined with trees and is unusually broad. It was famous for its stocking fairs, and it was also a centre for tanning and for the manufacture of Welsh flannel. It lies at the head of Bala Lake (Llyn Tegid), the largest natural lake in Wales, with a narrow-gauge railway running along its south-eastern shore. It is fringed round by imposing mountains, and is now a major watersports centre.

The White Lion is one of the most famous inns in the area. The present building has stood here since 1759, but there may well have been an older inn on this spot. Welsh whisky used to be casked behind the inn; Squire Price of the Rhiwlas Estate was the first to distil Welsh whisky hereabouts.

BALA, THE WHITE LION HOTEL, THE FISH ROOM BAR 1958 B7137

Borrow's breakfast

The White Lion was immortalised by the writer George Borrow, who enjoyed the most sumptuous breakfast of his life here in 1854 during the tour that he wrote of in 'Wild Wales' – 'a noble breakfast, such indeed as I might have read of but never before seen.' It included potted hare, potted trout, shrimps, local salmon, eggs, mutton chops, muffins, and a large loaf and butter, 'not forgetting capital tea'.

The Royal Oak Hotel, Betws-y-Coed

This famous resort on the Holyhead road, in the narrow, deeply-glaciated valley of the River Conwy, became popular when it was reached by the railway in Victorian times. Tourists then, as they do today, came to Betws for fishing and riding, and for walking among the mountains and waterfalls.

The artist David Cox painted the original signboard of this old coaching inn when he frequented Betws in the first half of the 19th century, painting the Machno Falls. N Neal Solly in his biography of David Cox tells the story: 'In the year 1847 Cox painted a sign-board in oil colours for the Royal Oak Inn – the subject, King Charles in the tree at Boscobel, with cavaliers on horseback galloping beneath, and dogs in the distance. Whilst he was busily employed in this position, a lady drove up – Mrs Ashley, an old pupil and acquaintance. Stopping her carriage, she greeted our artist, much to his astonishment, thus: "Oh, Mr Cox, is it really you! I hardly expected to see you here, mounted up so high on the ladder of fame". This signboard is now carefully varnished, and framed with twisted branches of oak from which the bark has been removed, and hangs on the right-hand side in the entrance hall. Cox's palette, which has been gilded, and brush, are placed over it. Two years after the sign was painted it wanted varnishing, and Cox, with his usual kindness, again mounted up on a ladder for this object.'

Betws-y-Coed

Below: BETWS-Y-COED, THE ROYAL OAK HOTEL 1892 30094

AMLWCH, DINORBEN SQUARE C1935   A274027

Amlwch

The Dinorben Arms and the Eleth Hotel, Amlwch

This narrow creek in the northern, rocky coast of Anglesey was an unlikely site for an important port, but the harbour developed as a result of extensive copper mining on Parys Mountain, two miles away – the mines were first worked by the Romans. This was once a busy port in the late 18th and 19th centuries; it was improved in 1793 and again in 1816 by the building of piers and wharves. Today, Amlwch is entirely devoted to the holiday trade.

The creeper-clad Dinorben Arms Hotel (left) and the Eleth Hotel (centre) provided good quality accommodation. The Dinorben was first listed as a hotel in 1828 when it was called the Ty Mawr; it was used as a courthouse before that. In 1784 it was recorded that a young man, William Roberts, was stripped to the waist, placed on horseback and flogged all the way to the port and back for stealing. The Eleth Hotel was demolished in 1962.

Denbigh

Cockfights to the death

Cockfighting was a very popular pastime in rural Wales until its prohibition in 1849. Cocks would be pitched against each other and set to fight to the death, accompanied by much raucous gambling. This old cockpit, built in the 17th century, survives today in the Museum of Welsh Life at St Fagans near Cardiff, where it was moved and re-constructed in 1970. Derelict by 1965, it was latterly used as a slaughterhouse and a garage.

The Hawk and Buckle Inn, Denbigh

This pleasant, stone-built market town on the western side of the lovely valley of Clwyd climbs the hillside crowned by its ruinous castle. The town has prospered from medieval times, and its market was vital in this growth. Farmers, traders and livestock have thronged Denbigh's streets from early times, and recent restoration works in the town are also revealing medieval buildings behind many of the seemingly later facades.

Above: DENBIGH, THE COCK PIT, THE HAWK AND BUCKLE INN C1955   D22120

The Chain Bridge Hotel, Llangollen

Llangollen has been a tourist centre since the 19th century; one of the principal attractions has been its canal spanning the Dee using Thomas Telford's marvel of the 121ft-high Froncysyllte Aqueduct, built in 1805. The town is most famous now for its annual international Eisteddfod. Other visitors are water sport enthusiasts heading for the River Dee.

Berwyn is a lonely spot west of Llangollen, where the half-timbered Chain Bridge Hotel and the station on the old Llangollen-Corwen railway stand beside the River Dee as it enters a small gorge. The waters race by and salmon leap. The Llangollen Canal begins its life just a short walk away at Horseshoe Falls, and vintage steam trains ply to and from the tiny station opposite the hotel. Today a huge modern extension has been built to the left of the old building. The chain bridge that gives its name to the hotel, a pioneering engineering feat, was built in 1814 by the wonderfully-named Exuperius Pickering to transport coal and lime from his mines from the canal to the road.

LLANGOLLEN,
THE CHAIN BRIDGE
HOTEL, BERWYN 1888
20681

Wrexham

WREXHAM, HOPE STREET AND THE TALBOT INN 1895 36284

The Talbot Inn, Wrexham. It is highly fitting that a book on inns should include Wrexham, for this was a brewery town. In the 19th century there were 19 breweries here, including the Wrexham Lager Brewery, founded in 1882, Britain's first lager brewery. The reason for all this brewing is the plentiful suitable water: the sands and gravels here filter the water that gathers on the impervious rocks below. In the coaching era, the town lay on the route of the Chester to Shrewsbury coach, which was notorious for being late. At last the stagecoach company discovered that the coach drivers would always stop at one of Wrexham's many inns for a prolonged drink. This photograph is particularly interesting in that it shows an earlier Talbot Inn than the present neo-Tudor half-timbered building that was erected in 1904–05. The Talbot we see here has windows that look Georgian, but does the rendering hide an earlier building?

Llangollen

Gatehouse of Fleet

The Anwoth Hotel, Gatehouse of Fleet

Gatehouse of Fleet, a charming town nestling in the valley of the River Fleet, is close to the beautiful Galloway coast with its sandy beaches, and behind it is a spectacular region of hills and mountains. The Anwoth Hotel has close associations with the detective story writer, playwright, and translator of Dante, Dorothy L Sayers. She and her husband stayed at the hotel in 1928, fell in love with the area, and later rented a house nearby. In her famous novel 'The Five Red Herrings' (1931), her detective Lord Peter Wimsey investigates the murder of a member of the local artistic community. The book lovingly depicts the landscape and the villages around Gatehouse, and it is dedicated to the then owner of the Anwoth Hotel, Joe Dignam. It is hard to believe today that Gatehouse used to be known as 'the Glasgow of the South'. Between 1750 and 1850 it was a thriving industrial town, with four cotton mills, a brewery, a brass foundry, tanneries, and a soap factory.

Left: GATEHOUSE OF FLEET, FLEET STREET, THE ANWOTH HOTEL C1955 G162019

Haddow's Temperance Hotel, Gourock. On the Firth of Clyde, this seaside resort looks across the Firth towards Kilcreggan, Loch Long and Dunoon. It is a centre for yachting and for boating trips in the Firth and to the Kyles of Bute, and a ferry terminal for Clydeside towns. It began life as a fishing village, but in the Victorian era it became a holiday resort, especially for Glaswegians.

The temperance movement was strongly supported in Scotland. John Dunlop, a local lawyer, was one of the leading lights in the Clydeside temperance movement, founding the first society in the 1820s. By 1876 the Independent Order of Good Templars had 84,000 members in Scotland, and an 1884 gazetteer tells us that at that time there were 'temperance and other societies' in Gourock. Small hotels like Haddow's would have been welcome to abstainers.

Gourock

GOUROCK, HADDOW'S TEMPERANCE HOTEL 1900 45985

Seeking Granny Kempock's blessing

On the cliff side of Gourock is a prehistoric monolith, Granny Kempoch's Stone; according to an 1884 gazetteer, sailors and fishermen 'would pace seven times around it, carrying a basketful of sea-sand and chanting an eerie strain, thereby to ensure a prosperous breeze; whilst a newly-wedded pair must also make the round of it, if they would have good luck.'

Ayr

The Tam O'Shanter Inn, Ayr

Famous as the birthplace of John Macadam in 1756 and of Robert Burns in 1759, Ayr was founded under a charter granted by William the Lion. This inn is the setting of Burns's mock-epic poem 'Tam O'Shanter': Tam and his crony Souter Johnny are much too fond of strong drink. After a night of hard drinking here, Tam sets off on his horse, Meg, only to be chased and tormented by all manner of supernatural horrors and witches. The witches nearly catch him, but just in time Tam remembers that they cannot cross running water, and spurs Meg on across the Brig o' Doon. He and Meg escape, but one of the witches, dressed in her 'cutty sark' (short dress), cuts off Meg's tail.

This poem is based on people who actually lived and drank here, Douglas Graham of Shanter Farm and his friend John Davidson (Souter Johnnie). Did Graham make up a similar tale as an excuse to his wife when he arrived home late after an evening's drinking? This inn became known as the Tam O'Shanter in the 19th century, when it was filled with Burns mementoes, and later it became a Burns museum. Today it is an inn once again.

Left: AYR, THE TAM O'SHANTER INN 1900
46005

The Woodside Hotel, Aberdour

Aberdour is a beautiful village on the coast of Fife looking across the Forth to Edinburgh. It has two beaches, a 13th-century castle, and a 12th-century church. The Woodside Hotel, in the centre of the village, is closely linked with the sea. The original owners, the Greig brothers of Inverkeithing, built the hotel in 1873; their grandfather shaped the Russian navy.

Since the Middle Ages, the Scots have seen Russia as a land of opportunity. Peter the Great's principal military advisor was General Patrick Gordon of Aberdeen, and Admiral Samuel Greig of Inverkeithing (1735–88), the father of the modern Russian navy, reformed the Baltic fleet for Catherine the Great and achieved resounding naval victory for her against the Turks at the battle of Chesme and the Swedes at the battle of Hogland. When he died, he was given a Russian state funeral. All four of his sons served in the Russian navy.

Another link between the Woodside Hotel and the sea is the ornate mahogany and glass ceiling in one room; this came from the SS 'Orontes', which used to ply between Britain and Australia in the 1920s.

Left: ABERDOUR, THE WOODSIDE HOTEL 1900   45911

Strathyre

STRATHYRE, THE STRATHYRE TEMPERANCE HOTEL C1915   44619A

Temperance Hotel, Strathyre. The name Strathyre means 'sheltered valley', and this beautiful, remote spot beside Loch Lubnaig is indeed sheltered by Ben Ledi, Ben Vane and Ben Shian. This village could be thought of as a gateway to the Highlands, for it nestles just north of the Pass of Leny at the fault line that demarcates the Highlands. The village grew up in the 1750s as a planned settlement for those who were attracted to the district by the opportunities offered by the new military road from Stirling to Fort William.

When the railway came through in 1870, it encouraged the building of hotels and villas to accommodate the tourists who were flocking to the Highlands. In the 18th century, Strathyre was nicknamed 'Nineveh' because it had so many inns; with the coming of the temperance movement in the 19th century, the demand grew for places for abstainers to stay. The size of this temperance hotel shows how very popular the movement was. Notice the charming young ladies with their boaters and bicycles – how hard was it to cycle in those long, voluminous skirts? How much harder would it have been if they had allowed themselves a tot of whisky?

Aberdeen

Castlegate, Aberdeen

The broad expanse of Castlegate lies at the heart of the city of Aberdeen, and has been the bustling market-place and centre of trade since the 12th century. The city's Mercat Cross, shown in the photograph, dates from the late 17th century. A market is always a strong focus for social drinking, with traders and their customers striking bargains in the bars and inns that line the street. In the background here we see a typical bar, plain and unassuming, but doubtless bustling with clientele on market days. Castlegate is now pedestrianised.

ABERDEEN, CASTLEGATE 1892 A90302Z

158

FREE PRINT OF YOUR CHOICE

Mounted Print
Overall size 14 x 11 inches (355 x 280mm)

CHOOSE A PHOTOGRAPH FROM THIS BOOK

Choose any Frith photograph in this book.

Simply complete the voucher opposite and return it with your remittance for £3.50
(to cover postage and handling) and we will print the photograph of your choice in SEPIA
(size 11 x 8 inches) and supply it in a cream mount with a burgundy rule line
(overall size 14 x 11 inches).

Offer valid for delivery to UK addresses only.

PLUS: **Order additional Mounted Prints at HALF PRICE - £8.50 each** (normally £17.00)
If you would like to order more Frith prints from this book, possibly as gifts for friends and
family, you can buy them at half price (with no additional postage and handling costs).

PLUS: **Have your Mounted Prints framed**
For an extra £14.95 per print you can have your mounted print(s) framed in an elegant
polished wood and gilt moulding, overall size 16 x 13 inches
(no additional postage and handling required).

IMPORTANT!

These special prices are only available if you use this form to order.

You must use the ORIGINAL VOUCHER on this page (no copies permitted).

We can only despatch to one UK address.

This offer cannot be combined with any other offer.

Send completed voucher form to:
The Francis Frith Collection, Frith's Barn, Teffont, Salisbury, Wiltshire SP3 5QP

Voucher *for FREE and Reduced Price Frith Prints*

Please do not photocopy this voucher. Only the original is valid, so please fill it in, cut it out and return it to us with your order.

Picture ref no	Page no	Qty	Mounted @ £8.50	Framed + £17.00	Total Cost £
		1	Free of charge*	£	£
			£8.50	£	£
			£8.50	£	£
			£8.50	£	£
			£8.50	£	£
			£8.50	£	£

Please allow 28 days for delivery.
Offer available to one UK address only

* Post & handling	£3.50
Total Order Cost	£

Title of this book. . . . .

I enclose a cheque/postal order for £ . . . .
made payable to 'The Francis Frith Collection'

OR please debit my Mastercard / Visa / Maestro card,
details below

Card Number

Issue No (Maestro only)   Valid from (Maestro)

Expires   Signature

Name Mr/Mrs/Ms . . . .
Address . . . .
. . . .
. . . .
. . . . Postcode . . . .
Daytime Tel No . . . .
Email . . . .

ISBN 0-7537-1444-2   Valid to 31/12/09

Can you help us with information about any of the Frith photographs in this book?

We are gradually compiling an historical record for each of the photographs in the Frith archive. It is always fascinating to find out the names of the people shown in the pictures, as well as insights into the shops, buildings and other features depicted.

If you recognize anyone in the photographs in this book, or if you have information not already included in the author's caption, visit the Frith website at www.francisfrith.com and add your memories.

Our production team

Frith books are produced by a small dedicated team at offices in the converted Grade II listed 18th-century barn at Teffont near Salisbury, illustrated above. Most have worked with The Francis Frith Collection for many years. All have in common one quality: they have a passion for The Francis Frith Collection. The team is constantly expanding, but currently includes:

Paul Baron, Jason Buck, John Buck, Jenny Coles, Heather Crisp, David Davies, Natalie Davis, Louis du Mont, Isobel Hall, Chris Hardwick, Neil Harvey, Julian Hight, Peter Horne, James Kinnear, Karen Kinnear, Tina Leary, Stuart Login, Sue Molloy, Sarah Roberts, Kate Rotondetto, Eliza Sackett, Terence Sackett, Sandra Sampson, Adrian Sanders, Sandra Sanger, Julia Skinner, Lewis Taylor, Will Tunnicliffe, David Turner and Ricky Williams.